CONTENTS

THE CONSOLIDATED FINANCIAL STATEMENTS OF THE FEDERAL GOVERNMENT FOR FISCAL YEAR 2002

HEARING

BEFORE THE

SUBCOMMITTEE ON GOVERNMENT EFFICIENCY AND FINANCIAL MANAGEMENT

OF THE

COMMITTEE ON GOVERNMENT REFORM

HOUSE OF REPRESENTATIVES

ONE HUNDRED EIGHTH CONGRESS

FIRST SESSION

APRIL 8, 2003

Serial No. 108–34

Printed for the use of the Committee on Government Reform

Available via the World Wide Web: http://www.gpo.gov/congress/house
http://www.house.gov/reform

U.S. GOVERNMENT PRINTING OFFICE

88–503 PDF WASHINGTON : 2003

For sale by the Superintendent of Documents, U.S. Government Printing Office
Internet: bookstore.gpo.gov Phone: toll free (866) 512–1800; DC area (202) 512–1800
Fax: (202) 512–2250 Mail: Stop SSOP, Washington, DC 20402–0001

COMMITTEE ON GOVERNMENT REFORM

TOM DAVIS, Virginia, *Chairman*

DAN BURTON, Indiana
CHRISTOPHER SHAYS, Connecticut
ILEANA ROS-LEHTINEN, Florida
JOHN M. McHUGH, New York
JOHN L. MICA, Florida
MARK E. SOUDER, Indiana
STEVEN C. LATOURETTE, Ohio
DOUG OSE, California
RON LEWIS, Kentucky
JO ANN DAVIS, Virginia
TODD RUSSELL PLATTS, Pennsylvania
CHRIS CANNON, Utah
ADAM H. PUTNAM, Florida
EDWARD L. SCHROCK, Virginia
JOHN J. DUNCAN, Jr., Tennessee
JOHN SULLIVAN, Oklahoma
NATHAN DEAL, Georgia
CANDICE S. MILLER, Michigan
TIM MURPHY, Pennsylvania
MICHAEL R. TURNER, Ohio
JOHN R. CARTER, Texas
WILLIAM J. JANKLOW, South Dakota
MARSHA BLACKBURN, Tennessee

HENRY A. WAXMAN, California
TOM LANTOS, California
MAJOR R. OWENS, New York
EDOLPHUS TOWNS, New York
PAUL E. KANJORSKI, Pennsylvania
CAROLYN B. MALONEY, New York
ELIJAH E. CUMMINGS, Maryland
DENNIS J. KUCINICH, Ohio
DANNY K. DAVIS, Illinois
JOHN F. TIERNEY, Massachusetts
WM. LACY CLAY, Missouri
DIANE E. WATSON, California
STEPHEN F. LYNCH, Massachusetts
CHRIS VAN HOLLEN, Maryland
LINDA T. SANCHEZ, California
C.A. "DUTCH" RUPPERSBERGER, Maryland
ELEANOR HOLMES NORTON, District of Columbia
JIM COOPER, Tennessee
CHRIS BELL, Texas

BERNARD SANDERS, Vermont (Independent)

PETER SIRH, *Staff Director*
MELISSA WOJCIAK, *Deputy Staff Director*
RANDY KAPLAN, *Senior Counsel/Parliamentarian*
TERESA AUSTIN, *Chief Clerk*
PHILIP M. SCHILIRO, *Minority Staff Director*

SUBCOMMITTEE ON GOVERNMENT EFFICIENCY AND FINANCIAL MANAGEMENT

TODD RUSSELL PLATTS, Pennsylvania, *Chairman*

MARSHA BLACKBURN, Tennessee
STEVEN C. LATOURETTE, Ohio
JOHN SULLIVAN, Oklahoma
CANDICE S. MILLER, Michigan
MICHAEL R. TURNER, Ohio

EDOLPHUS TOWNS, New York
PAUL E. KANJORSKI, Pennsylvania
MAJOR R. OWENS, New York
CAROLYN B. MALONEY, New York

EX OFFICIO

TOM DAVIS, Virginia

HENRY A. WAXMAN, California

MIKE HETTINGER, *Staff Director*
LARRY BRADY, *Professional Staff Member*
AMY LAUDEMAN, *Clerk*
MARK STEPHENSON, *Minority Professional Staff Member*

THE CONSOLIDATED FINANCIAL STATEMENTS OF THE FEDERAL GOVERNMENT FOR FISCAL YEAR 2002

TUESDAY, APRIL 8, 2003

HOUSE OF REPRESENTATIVES,
SUBCOMMITTEE ON GOVERNMENT EFFICIENCY AND FINANCIAL MANAGEMENT,
COMMITTEE ON GOVERNMENT REFORM,
Washington, DC.

The subcommittee met, pursuant to notice, at 10:38 a.m., in room 2203, Rayburn House Office Building, Hon. Todd Russell Platts (chairman of the subcommittee) presiding.

Present: Representatives Platts, Blackburn and Towns.

Staff present: Mike Hettinger, staff director; Dan Daly, counsel; Larry Brady and Kara Galles, professional staff members; Amy Laudeman, clerk; Mark Stephenson, minority professional staff member; and Christopher Davis, minority staff assistant.

Mr. PLATTS. The Subcommittee on Government Efficiency and Financial Management will come to order.

I appreciate everyone attending today and hope we enjoy the intimate setting we are in today as it is a little smaller room than normal.

Countless taxpayer dollars continue to be lost each year to fraud, waste and financial mismanagement in hundreds of Federal programs. In the subcommittee's last two hearings on the subject of "Governing with Accountability," we examined the President's Management Agenda, the Government Performance and Results Act [GPRA] and the Program Assessment Rating Tool [PART]. Each of those tools assists in improving financial management, but today we will look at the single most comprehensive statement of the status of the financial management of the Federal Government, the 2002 Financial Report of the U.S. Government.

The Financial Report and the accompanying audit of the report performed by the General Accounting Office were released on time as usual, on March 31, 2003. For the 6th straight year, GAO was unable to render an opinion on the Federal Government's financial statements. GAO reported significant material deficiencies that affected both the financial statements and the management of government operations.

For fiscal year 2002, an unprecedented 21 out of the 24 Chief Financial Officer Act agencies received unqualified or "clean" audit opinions on their individual financial statements. This is an improvement over 18 out of 24 agencies from fiscal year 2001. Only the Department of Defense, the Small Business Administration, and the U.S. Agency for International Development failed to receive clean opinions this year. GAO points out in their audit report of the consolidated statement that the financial management problems at DOD are "pervasive, complex, long-standing, and deeply rooted in virtually all business operations throughout the department." President Bush's administration has made improving financial performance a top priority, and I certainly commend the administration for their efforts. Secretary of Defense Donald Rumsfeld is working hard to improve DOD's financial management. With each fiscal year, DOD gets closer to obtaining an audit opinion. However, until DOD solves their financial problems and receives a clean opinion, the entire Federal Government's financial statement will continue to be unreliable.

Congress has placed a great deal of emphasis on the financial accountability of publicly traded companies and their responsibility to provide accurate information to investors. Congress and the Federal Government have an equal, if not greater responsibility, to be accountable to our investors, the American taxpayer.

Our witnesses today will shed light on the results of the consolidated financial statement and discuss areas that need improvement as well as financial management successes. Today, we are honored to have the Honorable David M. Walker who is the Comptroller General of the United States, who has just testified in the Senate; the Honorable Linda Springer, who is the Controller from the Office of Federal Financial Management at the Office of Management and Budget. I understand this is your first official testimony in your new position and we welcome you here today. I am going to use the chairman's privilege also as a proud son to recognize we have Ms. Springer's mom with us today to see her in action. We are delighted to have mom with us as well. We also have Donald V. Hammond, Fiscal Assistant Secretary, Department of Treasury. I look forward to your testimonies.

[The prepared statement of Hon. Todd Russell Platts follows:]

ONE HUNDRED EIGHTH CONGRESS

Congress of the United States

House of Representatives

COMMITTEE ON GOVERNMENT REFORM

2157 RAYBURN HOUSE OFFICE BUILDING

WASHINGTON, DC 20515–6143

MAJORITY (202) 225–5074
FACSIMILE (202) 225–3974
MINORITY (202) 225–5051
TTY (202) 225–6852

www.house.gov/reform

Opening Statement
Congressman Todd R. Platts
April 8, 2002

Countless taxpayer dollars continue to be lost each year to fraud, waste and financial mismanagement in hundreds of Federal programs. In the subcommittee's last two hearings on the subject of "Governing with Accountability," we examined the President's Management Agenda, the Government Performance and Results Act (GPRA) and Program Assessment Rating Tool (PART). Each of those tools assists in improving financial management, but today we will look at the single most comprehensive statement of the status of the financial management of the Federal government, the 2002 Financial Report of the United States Government.

The Financial Report and the accompanying audit of the report performed by the General Accounting Office (GAO) were released on time as usual, on March 31, 2003. For the sixth straight year, GAO was unable to render an opinion on the Federal government's financial statements. GAO reported significant material deficiencies that affected both the financial statements and the management of government operations.

For fiscal year 2002, an unprecedented 21 out of the 24 Chief Financial Officer Act agencies received unqualified or "clean" audit opinions on their individual financial statements. This is an improvement over 18 out of 24 agencies from fiscal year 2001. Only the Department of Defense, the Small Business Administration, and the United States Agency for International Development failed to receive clean opinions this year. GAO points out in their audit report of the consolidated statement that the financial management problems at DOD are "pervasive, complex, long-standing, and deeply rooted in virtually all business operations throughout the department." President Bush's Administration has made improving financial performance a top priority, and Secretary of Defense Donald Rumsfeld is working hard to improve DOD's financial management. With each fiscal year, DOD gets closer to obtaining an audit opinion. However, until DOD solves their financial problems and receives a clean opinion, the entire Federal government's financial statement will continue to be unreliable.

Congress has placed a great deal of emphasis on the financial accountability of publicly traded companies and their responsibility to provide accurate information to investors. Congress and the Federal government have an equal, if not greater responsibility, to be accountable to our investors, the American taxpayer.

Our witnesses today will shed light on the results of the consolidated financial statement and discuss areas that need improvement as well as financial management successes. Today, we are honored to have The Honorable David M. Walker who is the Comptroller General of the United States; The Honorable Linda Springer, who is the Controller from the Office of Federal Financial Management at the Office of Management and Budget; and Donald V. Hammond, Fiscal Assistant Secretary at the Department of Treasury. I look forward to your testimonies.

Mr. PLATTS. I am pleased to yield to the gentleman from New York, Mr. Towns, for the purpose of making an opening statement.

Mr. TOWNS. Thank you very much, Mr. Chairman.

Let me begin by saying this is a very important hearing. There is certainly a significant amount of good news in the General Accounting Office's audit of the Federal Government's finances. This year, the GAO was able to give 21 of the 24 agencies a clean audit opinion, up from 18 last year. We are moving in the right direction. However, to ensure that the entire Federal Government receives a clean audit, we must continue to pressure, cajole, persuade and encourage the executive branch agencies through hearings such as these.

Unfortunately, the prospect of all remaining agencies getting complete audits appear dim. The Comptroller General has described the financial management problem at DOD as pervasive, complex, longstanding and deeply rooted in virtually all business operations throughout the department. While it is probably difficult to divert additional resources at DOD to financial management systems during a time of war, we need to remember that correcting such management problems will make the department more effective in the long run and that we should not forget.

The Comptroller also noted weaknesses in financial systems throughout the executive branch. He specifically pointed out the Federal Government's inability to account for billions of dollars in transactions across government agencies. To overcome such problems, it seems apparent that we must replace all current stovepipe systems with the interoperable financial management solutions. We must also invest in the human capital in these agencies to understand and operate these systems. If the operation of financial systems of each agency is farmed out to different private companies, we will not be able to develop the day to day financial information system which we are seeking.

I look forward to hearing from our witnesses about the progress that has been made and what we need to do to overcome the remaining barriers to a consolidated financial statement of the Federal Government. We have come a long way but we still have a great distance to go.

On that note, Mr. Chairman, I yield.

Mr. PLATTS. Thank you, Mr. Towns.

I would now ask each witness and anyone who will be assisting you in the testimony you will provide to stand, raise your right hand and take the oath together. We will then proceed with the testimony.

[Witnesses sworn.]

Mr. PLATTS. Thank you. We will proceed now to testimony. Mr. Walker, we will begin with you. We appreciate your racing over from the Senate. Hopefully you have had a chance to catch your breath before starting. We will then proceed to Ms. Springer and Mr. Hammond.

We appreciate the substantive detailed testimony in writing you all provided to the committee which allowed us a chance to review it prior to today's hearing and please summarize that as best you can. Because of the detail and importance of the information you are covering today, we would extend to each of you 10 minutes for your opening statements. Then we will go to questions.

Mr. Walker.

STATEMENTS OF DAVID M. WALKER, COMPTROLLER GENERAL OF THE UNITED STATES, U.S. GENERAL ACCOUNTING OFFICE; LINDA M. SPRINGER, CONTROLLER, OFFICE OF FEDERAL FINANCIAL MANAGEMENT, OFFICE OF MANAGEMENT AND BUDGET; AND DONALD V. HAMMOND, FISCAL ASSISTANT SECRETARY, DEPARTMENT OF THE TREASURY

Mr. WALKER. Thank you, Mr. Chairman and members of the subcommittee. I appreciate your understanding. I literally ran from a joint Senate/House hearing. I am glad I am in good shape because otherwise I may not have made it.

I appreciate also being able to put the entire statement in the record and being able to summarize the key portions.

I am pleased to be here today to discuss our report on the U.S. Government's consolidated financial statements for fiscal years 2002 and 2001. As in the 5 previous fiscal years, certain material weaknesses in internal control and in accounting and reporting prevented us from being able to provide the Congress and American citizens an opinion as to whether the consolidated financial statements are fairly stated in conformity with U.S. generally accepted accounting principles.

Across government, financial management improvement initiatives are under way that, if effectively implemented, have the potential to appreciably improve the quality of the Federal Government's financial management and reporting. You, Mr. Chairman, and members of the subcommittee know I have a 15 year term. I am now 4½ years into my term and I hope and expect that by the end of my term, there will be a clean opinion on the Government's financial statements. I underline I hope and expect but there is a lot of work that needs to be done to get us there.

For fiscal year 2002, 21 of the 24 CFO Act agencies were able to attain unqualified audit opinions on their financial statements, up from 6 agencies for fiscal year 1996. Also, 4 CFO Act agencies showed improvement by receiving unqualified opinions from their auditors this year.

Although obtaining unqualified audit opinions is important, according to the President's Management Agenda, "most Federal agencies that obtain clean audits only do so after making extraordinary, labor-intensive assaults on financial records." I have referred to this in past years as "heroic efforts" to basically be able to recreate the books at the end of the year several months after the end of the year. I question the prudence or appropriateness of doing that, which is why, as I will note in a few minutes, the JFMIP Principles have agreed to a number of steps that will help to assure this does not occur in the future and that these opinions are truly earned and not created due to significant expenditures or human resource commitments that are questionable.

Before discussing the results of the audit of the U.S. Government's consolidated financial statements in more detail, I would like to discuss why sound financial management is especially necessary for the future, as well as for today, to meet tomorrow's challenges. I have on the chart the latest 50 year, long-range budget simulation results from GAO's analysis, which we do twice a year and have been doing for about 10 years.

It shows that based upon current tax revenues as a percentage of the economy, based upon projected spending by the Social Security and Medicare trustees, their best estimate, and assuming that discretionary spending grows at the rate of the economy, if you assume all that is true, this is what the future looks like on autopilot. Starting in less than 10 years, the current deficits start escalating very rapidly due primarily to known demographic trends and rising health care costs to levels that we have never seen before.

As a result, it is critically important that we start reviewing all existing Federal programs and policies—spending, tax incentives, regulatory, and otherwise—to basically answer three fundamental questions. What should the Federal Government be doing in the 21st century, how should the Federal Government do business in the 21st century and, in some cases, who should do the Government's business in the 21st century?

The current base is unsustainable. We have to make tough choices and in order to make those tough choices, it will be important to have timely, accurate, and useful financial and cost information to be able to make informed choices that are going to be difficult but nonetheless necessary.

The next chart shows a range of existing commitments, liabilities, and contingencies that we already have. In some cases, these amounts are noted as liabilities in the consolidated financial statements of the U.S. Government; in some cases they are not and may not ever be but they are huge. We have publicly held debt which is a liability of $3.54 trillion. We also have a significant amount of Government-held debt, debt held in trust funds like Social Security and Medicare which are backed by an unconditional promise to pay from the Federal Government, $2.67 trillion but it is where the right hand owes the left hand, so poof, it is gone on the consolidated financial statements of the U.S. Government. It is not currently shown as a liability.

Furthermore, we have significant differences between projected revenues and projected expenditures under a number of programs, such as Social Security and Medicare, where the discounted present value of that difference amounts to almost $10 trillion just in Social Security and Medicare Part A alone. In other words, you would have to have $10 trillion invested at Treasury rates today just to be able to fund the gap between promised benefits and estimated revenues. These gaps are huge. And by the way, these gaps only cover 75 years and are growing every year. So it is important that we recognize that we are on an unsustainable path, that tough choices will have to be made, not only with regard to entitlement programs but also with regard to discretionary spending and, in some cases, with regard to certain tax incentives. Frankly some tax incentives may not be doing what we would like them to do as it relates to policy, such as, for example, health care tax incentives, on which I will answer questions on if you like. Having sound financial management systems is important to understanding these issues and making tough choices.

As I mentioned earlier, as has been the case for the past 5 years, the Federal Government continues to have a significant number of material weaknesses related to financial statements, the fundamental recordkeeping and financial reporting problems and incomplete documentation. Several of these material weaknesses resulted in conditions that prevented us from being able to express an opinion.

The three major impediments to GAO being able to express an opinion on the consolidated financial statements are: (1) the serious financial management problems at DOD, although they are making progress; (2) the Federal Government's continued inability to fully account for and reconcile billions of dollars of transactions between Federal Government departments and agencies; and (3) the Federal Government's inability to properly prepare consolidated financial statements.

Over the past year, the JFMIP Principals, which I had the privilege to chair for a 2-year period ending last September 30, began an effort to accelerate progress in financial reform that involved a personal commitment of each of the principals to provide leadership in this critical area. Since August 2001, the JFMIP Principals have established an excellent working relationship and basis for action, a new sense of urgency in this area through which significant and meaningful progress has been achieved and continues to be achieved.

In fiscal year 2002, we had a series of regular deliberative meetings and took a number of steps outlined on page 20 of my testimony. The continued personal involvement of the principals is critical to full and successful implementation of financial management reforms. I would add it is also critical that this subcommittee and others in Congress continue to hold oversight hearings in order for us to continue to make progress. This subcommittee has been fantastic over the last several years in making sure everybody is focused on continually making progress.

Building on the success that has been achieved in obtaining unqualified opinions, Federal agency management must continue to work to fully resolve the pervasive and generally longstanding material weaknesses we have reported. Irrespective of the unqualified opinions in their financial statements, many Federal agencies do not have sound controls along with timely, accurate, and useful financial information and sound controls with which to make informed decisions and ensure accountability on a day-to-day basis.

Two audit matters have come to the fore in the last year that are key to protecting the public interest. One matter involves auditor responsibilities for reporting internal control and the other concerns auditor independence. GAO has led by example in these two areas, not only within the Government but also within the accountability profession at large. We are committed to continue to do so.

In closing, Mr. Chairman and members, our report on the U.S. Government's consolidated financial statements for fiscal years 2001 and 2002 highlights the need to continue addressing the Government's serious financial management weaknesses. The requirement for timely, accurate, and useful financial and performance information is greater than ever as the Congress and the administration prepare to meet our growing fiscal challenges.

Finally, I want to reiterate the value of sustained congressional interest in these issues as demonstrated by this hearing and by the sustained commitment of this subcommittee.

Thank you, Mr. Chairman. I would be happy to answer questions after my colleagues have their chance to read their testimony.

[The prepared statement of Mr. Walker follows:]

United States General Accounting Office

GAO

Testimony

Before the Subcommittee on Government Efficiency and Financial Management, Committee on Government Reform, House of Representatives

For Release on Delivery
Expected at 10:30 a.m.
Tuesday, April 8, 2003

FISCAL YEAR 2002 U.S. GOVERNMENT FINANCIAL STATEMENTS

Sustained Leadership and Oversight Needed for Effective Implementation of Financial Management Reform

Statement of David M. Walker
Comptroller General of the United States

GAO
Accountability • Integrity • Reliability

GAO-03-572T

April 8, 2003

GAO
Accountability·Integrity·Reliability

Highlights

Highlights of GAO-03-572T, testimony before the Subcommittee on Government Efficiency and Financial Management, Committee on Government Reform, House of Representatives

Why GAO Did This Study

GAO is required by law to audit the consolidated financial statements of the U.S. government.

Timely, accurate, and useful financial information is essential for making informed operating decisions day to day, managing the federal government's operations more efficiently and effectively, meeting the goals of federal financial management reform legislation, supporting results-oriented management approaches, and ensuring accountability on an ongoing basis.

The importance of such information is heightened by the unprecedented demographic challenge of an aging population. Federal spending on the elderly, health care, and new homeland security and defense commitments increases the need to look at competing claims on the budget and at new priorities.

Over the past year, the Principals of the Joint Financial Management Improvement Program continued efforts to accelerate progress in financial management reform. Also, President Bush has implemented the President's Management Agenda to provide direction to, and closely monitor, management reform across government, which encompasses improved financial management performance. To effectively implement federal financial management reform, sustained leadership and oversight are essential.

www.gao.gov/cgi-bin/getrpt?GAO-03-572T.

To view the full report, including the scope and methodology, click on the link above. For more information, contact Jeffrey Steinhoff or Gary Engel at (202) 512-2600.

FISCAL YEAR 2002 U.S. GOVERNMENT FINANCIAL STATEMENTS

Sustained Leadership and Oversight Needed for Effective Implementation of Financial Management Reform

What GAO Found

As in the 5 previous fiscal years, the federal government continues to have a significant number of material weaknesses related to financial systems, fundamental recordkeeping and financial reporting, and incomplete documentation. Several of these material weaknesses resulted in conditions that continued to prevent us from expressing an opinion on the U.S. government's consolidated financial statements for the fiscal years ended September 30, 2002 and 2001.

Three major impediments to an opinion on the consolidated financial statements are (1) serious financial management problems at DOD, (2) the federal government's inability to fully account for and reconcile billions of dollars of transactions between federal entities, and (3) the federal government's inability to properly prepare the consolidated financial statements.

Federal agencies have continued to make progress in obtaining unqualified audit opinions—21 of 24 Chief Financial Officers (CFO) Act agencies for fiscal year 2002 (see table), up from 6 for fiscal year 1996. Irrespective of the unqualified opinions, many federal agencies do not have timely, accurate, and useful financial information and sound controls with which to make informed decisions and to ensure accountability on an ongoing basis.

Building on the success achieved in obtaining unqualified audit opinions, federal agency management must continue to work toward fully resolving the pervasive and generally long-standing material weaknesses that have been reported for the past 6 fiscal years. The President's Management Agenda stated that without sound internal control and accurate and timely financial information, it is not possible to accomplish the President's agenda to secure the best performance and highest measure of accountability for the American people.

Fiscal Year 2002 CFO Act Agency Results Reported by Auditors

Agencies with unqualified opinions	Agencies with unqualified opinions and no material weaknesses or noncompliances
21[a]	4[b]

Source: GAO.

[a] Agriculture, Commerce, Education, Energy, Federal Emergency Management Agency, Health and Human Services, Housing and Urban Development, Interior, Justice, Labor, State, Transportation, Treasury, Veterans Affairs, Environmental Protection Agency, General Services Administration, National Aeronautics and Space Administration, National Science Foundation, Nuclear Regulatory Commission, Office of Personnel Management, and Social Security Administration.

[b] Energy, General Services Administration, National Science Foundation, and Social Security Administration.

Mr. Chairman and Members of the Subcommittee:

I am pleased to be here today to discuss our report on the U.S. government's consolidated financial statements for fiscal years 2002 and 2001. Both the consolidated financial statements and our report are included in the fiscal year 2002 *Financial Report of the United States Government*, which was issued by the Department of the Treasury (Treasury) on March 31, 2003, and is available through GAO's Internet site, at www.gao.gov, and Treasury's Internet site, at www.fms.treas.gov/fr/index.html. At the outset, I would like to thank the subcommittee for continuing an annual tradition of oversight hearings on this important subject. The work of the former Subcommittee on Government Efficiency, Financial Management, and Intergovernmental Relations, along with its leader, former Congressman Stephen Horn, has been a catalyst to facilitate government management reform over the past 6 years. The continued involvement of this subcommittee will be critical to ultimately restoring public confidence in the federal government as a financial steward that is accountable for its finances.

As in the 5 previous fiscal years, certain material weaknesses[1] in internal control and in accounting and reporting prevented us from being able to provide the Congress and American citizens an opinion as to whether the consolidated financial statements are fairly stated in conformity with U.S. generally accepted accounting principles. Until the problems discussed in our report are adequately addressed, they will continue to (1) hamper the federal government's ability to accurately report a significant portion of its assets, liabilities, and costs, (2) affect the federal government's ability to accurately measure the full cost and financial performance of certain programs and effectively manage related operations, and (3) significantly impair the federal government's ability to adequately safeguard certain significant assets and properly record various transactions.

Across government, financial management improvement initiatives are under way that, if effectively implemented, have the potential to appreciably improve the quality of the federal government's financial management and reporting. A number of federal agencies have started to

[1]A material weakness is a condition that precludes the entity's internal control from providing reasonable assurance that misstatements, losses, or noncompliance material in relation to the financial statements or to stewardship information would be prevented or detected on a timely basis.

make progress in their efforts to modernize their financial management systems and improve financial management performance as called for in the President's Management Agenda. For example, the Department of the Treasury's Internal Revenue Service (IRS) has made significant progress in addressing its financial management weaknesses, including addressing controls over budgetary activity and its accountability over property and equipment. Resolving many of IRS's most serious financial management weaknesses—identified by GAO as a high-risk area since 1995—will require a sustained, long-term commitment of resources, continued strong involvement of senior IRS management, and sustained progress in systems modernization.

This year marks the earliest that federal agencies' audited financial statements have ever been available. For the first time, Chief Financial Officers Act (CFO) Act agencies were required to combine their audited financial statements with performance reports and deliver both to the Office of Management and Budget (OMB) by February 1, a month earlier than last year. Furthermore, the Principals of the Joint Financial Management Improvement Program (JFMIP)[2]—the Secretary of the Treasury, the Directors of OMB and the Office of Personnel Management (OPM), and I, as Comptroller General of the United States—have agreed to accelerate the agency financial statement reporting date to November 15 for fiscal year 2004. The Social Security Administration (SSA), which has a long-standing record of delivering its audited financial statements well before the mandated deadline, issued its fiscal year 2002 audited financial statements on November 19, 2002. Treasury also accelerated its time frame and issued its fiscal year 2002 audited financial statements on November 15, 2002, which was more than 3 months earlier than for fiscal year 2001.

For fiscal year 2002, 21 of the 24 CFO Act agencies were able to attain unqualified audit opinions on their financial statements (the appendix lists the 24 CFO Act agencies, their audit results, and auditors), up from 6 agencies for fiscal year 1996. Also, 4 CFO Act agencies showed improvement by receiving unqualified opinions from their auditors this year—the Department of Education, the National Aeronautics and Space Administration (NASA), the Federal Emergency Management Agency, and

[2]JFMIP is a joint and cooperative undertaking of Treasury, GAO, OMB, and OPM working in cooperation with each other and other federal agencies to improve financial management practices in the federal government. Leadership and program guidance are provided by the four JFMIP Principals.

the Department of Agriculture (USDA), which received an unqualified audit opinion for the first time. On the other hand, after receiving unqualified opinions on its financial statements since fiscal year 1996, the Small Business Administration's (SBA) independent auditor withdrew its unqualified audit opinions on the agency's fiscal years 2001 and 2000 financial statements and issued disclaimers of opinion on the agency's fiscal years 2002 and 2001 financial statements.

Although obtaining unqualified audit opinions is important, according to the President's Management Agenda, "most federal agencies that obtain clean audits only do so after making extraordinary, labor-intensive assaults on financial records." Further, the President's Management Agenda stated that without sound internal control and accurate and timely financial information, it is not possible to accomplish the President's agenda to secure the best performance and highest measure of accountability for the American people. It will be increasingly difficult for federal agencies to continue to rely on significant costly and time-intensive manual efforts to achieve or maintain unqualified opinions until automated, integrated processes and systems are implemented that readily produce the necessary information. As a result, many federal agencies must accelerate their efforts to improve underlying financial management systems and controls, which is consistent with reaching the financial management success measures envisioned by the JFMIP Principals and called for by the President's Management Agenda.

Before discussing the results of the audit of the U.S. government's consolidated financial statements in more detail, I would like to discuss why sound financial management is especially necessary for the future, as well as for today, to meet tomorrow's fiscal needs. I then will highlight the major issues relating to the consolidated financial statements for fiscal years 2002 and 2001. I will then discuss the urgency of providing sustained leadership and oversight for effective implementation of financial management reform, provide my perspectives on the importance of federal agencies' building on the success of their unqualified audit opinions by significantly improving underlying financial management systems, and underscore the need to address major impediments to an opinion on the consolidated financial statements. Also, I will present my observations on selected audit matters that are key to protecting the public interest.

Meeting Tomorrow's Fiscal Needs

The requirement for timely, accurate, and useful financial and performance management information is greater than ever. The long-term fiscal pressures created by the retirement of the baby boom generation and new homeland security and defense commitments, including the ongoing Operation Iraqi Freedom, sharpen the need to look at competing claims on federal budgetary resources and new priorities. In previous testimony, I noted that it should be the norm to reconsider the relevance or "fit" of any federal program or activity in today's world and for the future.[3] Such a fundamental review is necessary both to increase fiscal flexibility and to make government fit the modern world. Stated differently, there is a need to consider what the proper role of the federal government will be in the 21st century and how the government should do business in the future. The budget and performance integration initiative undertaken as part of the President's Management Agenda should help provide information for use in conducting such reviews. OMB's Program Assessment Rating Tool (PART) represents a step toward more structured involvement of program and performance analysis in the budget. PART includes general questions on (1) program purpose and design, (2) strategic planning, (3) program management, and (4) program results. It also includes a set of more specific questions that vary according to the type of delivery mechanism or approach the program uses.

As we look ahead, the federal government faces an unprecedented demographic challenge. A nation that has prided itself on its youth will become older. Between now and 2035, the number of people who are 65 years old or over will double. As the share of the population over 65 climbs, federal spending on the elderly will absorb larger and ultimately unsustainable shares of the federal budget. Federal spending on health and entitlement programs for the elderly is expected to surge as people live longer and spend more time in retirement. In addition, advances in medical technology are likely to keep pushing up the cost of providing health care. Moreover, the baby boomers will have left behind fewer workers to support them in retirement, prompting a slower rate of economic growth from which to finance these higher costs. Absent substantive reform of related entitlement programs and/or dramatic changes in tax or discretionary spending policies, we will face large, escalating, and persistent deficits.

[3] U.S. General Accounting Office, *Budget Issues: Long-Term Fiscal Challenges*, GAO-02-467T (Washington, D.C.: Feb. 27, 2002) and U.S. General Accounting Office, *Budget Issues: Effective Oversight and Budget Discipline are Essential—Even in a Time of Surplus*, GAO/T-AIMD-00-73 (Washington, D.C.: Feb. 1, 2000).

These trends have widespread implications for our society, our economy, and the federal budget.

On March 17, 2003, the Trustees of the Social Security and Medicare trust funds reported on the current and projected status of these programs over the next 75 years. The Trustees report that the fundamentals of the financial status of both Social Security and Medicare remain highly problematic. However, they stated that Medicare faces financial difficulties that are more severe than those confronting Social Security because costs of the Medicare program are projected to rise faster than costs of the Social Security program. The projections show a 20 percent increase to about $6.2 trillion over the prior year in the Present Value of Resources Needed Over the 75-Year Projection Period for Federal Hospital Insurance (Medicare Part A), while the Social Security projection showed an 8 percent increase to about $4.9 trillion. Once again, the Trustees state that action to address the financial difficulties facing Social Security and Medicare must be taken in a timely manner and that the sooner these financial challenges are addressed, the more varied and less disruptive the solutions can be.

Early action to change these programs would yield the highest fiscal dividends for the federal budget and would provide a longer period for prospective beneficiaries to make adjustments in their own planning. Waiting to take action entails risks. First, we lose an important window where today's relatively large workforce can increase saving and enhance productivity, two elements critical to growing the future economy. Second, we lose the opportunity to reduce the burden of interest in the federal budget, thereby creating a legacy of higher debt as well as elderly entitlement spending for the relatively smaller workforce of the future. Third, and most critically, we risk losing the opportunity to phase in changes gradually so that all can make the adjustments needed in private and public plans to accommodate this historic shift.

We prepare long-term budget simulations that seek to illustrate the likely fiscal consequences of the coming demographic tidal wave and rising health care costs. Our latest long-term budget simulations reinforce the need for change in the major cost drivers—Social Security and health care programs. As shown in figure 1, by midcentury, absent reform of these entitlement programs, projected federal revenues may be adequate to pay little beyond interest on the debt and Social Security benefits. Further, the shift from surplus to deficit means that the nation will move into the future in a weaker fiscal position than was previously the case.

Figure 1:

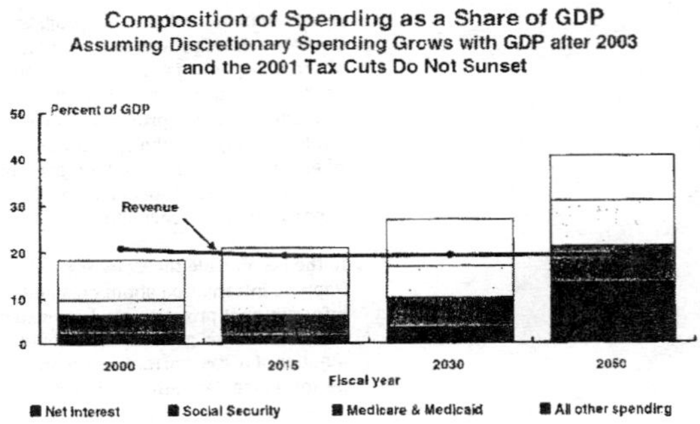

Source: GAO's March 2003 analysis.

Note: Assumes currently scheduled Social Security benefits are paid in full throughout the simulation period.

Although the need for structural change in Social Security is widely recognized, this change would not be sufficient to overcome the long-term fiscal challenges confronting the nation. For example, the long-term fiscal imbalance would not come close to being eliminated even if Social Security benefits were to be limited to currently projected trust fund revenues, because Medicare and Medicaid—spending for which is driven by both demographics and rising health care costs—present an even greater problem.

While addressing the challenges of Social Security and Medicare is key to ensuring future fiscal flexibility, a fundamental review of major programs, policies, and operations can create much-needed fiscal flexibility to address emerging needs. As I have stated previously, it is healthy for the nation periodically to review and update its programs, activities, and priorities.[4] Many federal programs and policies were designed years ago to respond to earlier challenges. Ultimately, the federal government should strive to hand to the next generation the legacy of a government that is effective and relevant to a changing society—a government that is as free as possible of outmoded commitments and operations that can inappropriately encumber the future.

A reexamination of existing programs and policies could help weed out items that have proven to be outdated or persistently ineffective or alternatively could prompt us to update and modernize activities through such actions as improving program targeting and efficiency, consolidation, or reengineering of processes and operations. Such a review should not be limited to only spending programs but should include the full range of tools of governance that the federal government uses to address national objectives. These tools include loans and loan guarantees, tax expenditures, and regulations.

In the last decade the Congress put in place a series of laws designed to improve information about cost and performance. This framework and the information it provides can help structure and inform the debate about what the federal government should do. In addition, GAO has identified a number of areas warranting reconsideration based on program performance, targeting, and costs.

The events of the past few years have served to highlight the benefits of fiscal flexibility. Addressing the long-term drivers in the budget is essential to preserving any flexibility in the long term. In the nearer term, a fundamental review of existing programs and policies can also create much-needed fiscal flexibility. In this regard, the federal government must determine how best to address the necessary structural challenges in a reasonably timely manner in order to identify specific actions that need to be taken. As steward of the nation's future, the federal government must begin to prepare for tomorrow.

Need for New Metrics and Mechanisms

Today's budget decisions shape, in part, the choices and resources available to future decision makers and taxpayers. Accordingly, today's budget decisions involve tradeoffs between meeting current needs and fulfilling stewardship responsibilities. The government undertakes a wide range of responsibilities, programs, and activities that may call for future spending or create an expectation for such spending. Figure 2 illustrates some of these claims on future federal resources.

[4] GAO/T-AIMD-00-73.

Figure 2:

Selected Fiscal Exposures: Sources and Example
(End of Fiscal Year 2002)

Type	Example (dollars in billions)
Explicit liabilities	• Publicly held debt ($3,540) • Military & civilian pension & post-retirement health ($2,673) • Veterans benefits payable ($849) • Environmental and disposal liabilities ($273) • Loan guarantees ($28)
Explicit financial commitments	• Undelivered orders ($539) • Long-term leases ($50)
Explicit financial contingencies	• Unadjudicated claims ($9) • National insurance programs ($43)
Implicit exposures implied by current policies or the public's expectations about the role of government	• Debt held by government accounts ($2,674) • Future Social Security benefit payments ($3,549)* • Future Medicare Part A benefit payments ($5,931)* • Life cycle costs including deferred & future maintenance and operating costs (amount unknown)

Source: GAO.

*These amounts represent NPV over 75 years and are net of debt held by the Trust Funds ($1,378 billion for Social Security and $235 billion for Medicare Part A). Figures for Social Security and Medicare Part A are as of January 1, 2003.

A better understanding and more transparency about these "fiscal exposures" is needed. The budget needs to employ new metrics and measures and processes—relying more on long-term estimates and present value concepts in making resource allocation decisions. Neither current budget reporting nor financial statements are designed to promote the recognition and explicit consideration of all of these exposures. Our nation's fiscal exposures cover a wide range: from explicit liabilities to implicit promises embedded in current policy or public expectations. Some, like accounts payable and loan guarantees, are included in both the budget and financial statements and some are not. Others, such as liability for environmental cleanup, are reported in the financial statements, but only a single year's figures are in the budget. Some implicit exposures, such as future Social Security and Medicare benefits, are not included in the budget or reported as liabilities in the financial statements[5] but are captured in long-range budget projections. Other implicit exposures, such as the risk assumed by insurance programs, may not be captured in either budget or financial reporting.

The failure to understand and address these fiscal exposures can have significant consequences, encumbering future budgets and reducing fiscal flexibility. Further, the failure to capture the long-term costs of a proposal or decision limits the Congress's ability to control fiscal exposures at the time it is being asked to make the decision.

As the figure makes clear, there is wide diversity in the nature of these fiscal exposures. This diversity suggests that it would be most useful to look at different types of fiscal exposures and tailor metrics and changes to address each type. We recently recommended[6] that OMB report annually on fiscal exposures, including a concise list and description and cost estimates where possible. We also recommended that, where possible, OMB report the estimated costs associated with certain exposures as a new budget concept—"exposure level"—as a notational item in the President's budget. These two steps would help alert both the public and policy makers about the long-term implications of programs, policies and activities.

[5]The stewardship information section of the U.S. government's consolidated financial statements presents the present value of long-range actuarial projections for the Social Security and Medicare programs, together with related information.

[6]U.S. General Accounting Office, *Fiscal Exposures: Improving the Budgetary Focus on Long-Term Costs and Uncertainties*, GAO-03-213 (Washington, D.C.: Jan. 24, 2003).

It is important to recognize that for trust funds, greater transparency and fuller disclosure means going beyond trust fund balances or solvency measures. For federal trust funds the balances do not provide meaningful information about program sustainability. These balances do not increase the government's ability to meet long-term commitments. Nor do they necessarily represent the full future cost of existing promises. For example, the projected exhaustion date of the Hospital Insurance (HI) Trust Fund is a commonly used indicator of HI's financial condition. Under the Trustees' 2003 intermediate estimates, the HI Trust Fund is projected to exhaust its assets in 2026. Long before that, however, HI's program outlays will exceed program tax revenues. Under the Trustees' 2003 intermediate estimates, this will begin in 2013. To finance program cash deficits, HI will need to draw on the special-issue Treasury securities acquired during the years of cash surpluses. For HI to "redeem" its securities, the government will need to obtain cash through some combination of increased taxes, spending cuts, and/or increased borrowing from the public (or, if the unified budget is in surplus, less debt reduction than would otherwise have been the case). HI's negative cash flow will place increased pressure on the federal budget to raise the resources necessary to meet the program's ongoing costs.

Ultimately, the critical question is not how much a trust fund has in assets, but whether the government as a whole and the economy can afford the promised benefits now and in the future and at what cost to other claims on available resources. Extending a trust fund's solvency without reforms to make the underlying program more sustainable can create a false sense of security and delay needed reform. Because the balances can be misleading, we need to reconsider how trust funds, and the nonmarketable federal government securities contained therein, are treated in both the budget and the federal government's financial statements.

Today the Congress and President Bush face the challenge of sorting out these many claims on the federal budget without the budget enforcement mechanisms or fiscal benchmarks that guided the federal government through the years of deficit reduction.[7] However, it is still the case that the federal government needs a decision-making framework that permits it to evaluate choices against both today's needs and the longer-term fiscal future that will be handed to future generations. More complete, visible,

[7]We have recently issued a report offering some suggestions on how to better improve information about the long-term cost implications of various programs and activities. See GAO-03-213.

and transparent reporting of fiscal exposures can better position decision makers to do this.

Highlights of Major Issues Relating to the U.S. Government's Consolidated Financial Statements for Fiscal Years 2002 and 2001

As I mentioned earlier, as has been the case for the past 5 fiscal years, the federal government continues to have a significant number of material weaknesses related to financial systems, fundamental recordkeeping and financial reporting, and incomplete documentation. Several of these material weaknesses (referred to hereafter as material deficiencies) resulted in conditions that continued to prevent us from expressing an opinion on the U.S. government's consolidated financial statements for the fiscal years ended September 30, 2002 and 2001.[8] There may also be additional issues that could affect the consolidated financial statements that have not been identified.

Major challenges include the federal government's inability to

- properly account for and report property, plant, and equipment and inventories and related property, primarily at the Department of Defense (DOD);
- reasonably estimate or adequately support amounts reported for certain liabilities, such as environmental and disposal liabilities and related costs at DOD, and ensure complete and proper reporting for commitments and contingencies;
- support major portions of the total net cost of government operations, most notably related to DOD, and ensure that all disbursements are properly recorded;
- fully account for and reconcile intragovernmental activity and balances; and
- properly prepare the federal government's financial statements, including fully ensuring that the information in the consolidated financial statements is consistent with the underlying agency financial statements, balancing the statements, adequately reconciling the results

[8] We previously reported that material deficiencies prevented us from expressing an opinion on the fiscal years 1997, 1998, 1999, and 2000 consolidated financial statements.

of operations to budget results, and eliminating transactions between governmental entities.

In addition, we identified material weaknesses in internal control related to loans receivable and loan guarantee liabilities, improper payments, tax collection activities, and information security.

I would now like to discuss in more detail the material deficiencies identified by our work.

Property, Plant, and Equipment and Inventories and Related Property

The federal government could not satisfactorily determine that all such assets were included in the consolidated financial statements, verify that certain reported assets actually exist, or substantiate the amounts at which they were valued. A significant portion of the property, plant, and equipment and the vast majority of inventories and related property are the responsibility of DOD. DOD did not maintain adequate systems or have sufficient records to provide reliable information on these assets. Other agencies, most notably NASA, reported continued weaknesses in internal control procedures and processes related to property, plant, and equipment.

Liabilities and Commitments and Contingencies

The federal government could not reasonably estimate or adequately support amounts reported for certain liabilities. For example, the federal government was not able to reliably estimate key components of DOD's environmental and disposal liabilities and could not support its estimate of military postretirement health benefits liabilities included in federal employee and veteran benefits payable. Further, the federal government could not determine whether commitments and contingencies, including those related to treaties and other agreements entered into to further the U.S. government's interest, were complete and properly reported.

Cost of Government Operations and Disbursement Activity

The previously discussed material deficiencies in reporting assets and liabilities, material deficiencies in financial statement preparation, as discussed below, and the lack of adequate disbursement reconciliations at certain federal agencies affect reported net costs. As a result, the federal government was unable to support significant portions of the total net cost of government operations, most notably related to DOD. As it relates to disbursement reconciliations, some federal agencies did not adequately reconcile disbursements to Treasury's records of disbursements, which is intended to be a key control to detect and correct errors and other misstatements in financial records in a timely manner. We have seen progress in this area over the past 6 years. However, for fiscal years 2002 and 2001 there were unsupported adjustments and unreconciled differences between federal agencies' and Treasury's records of disbursements totaling billions of dollars.

Accounting for and Reconciliation of Intragovernmental Activity and Balances

OMB and Treasury require CFO Act agencies to reconcile selected intragovernmental activity and balances with their "trading partners"[9] and to report on the extent and results of intragovernmental activity and balances reconciliation efforts. However, a substantial number of the CFO Act agencies did not fully perform such reconciliations for fiscal years 2002 and 2001. For both of these years, amounts reported for federal agency trading partners for certain intragovernmental accounts were significantly out of balance. I will discuss these issues further later in this testimony, as well as certain related corrective actions being taken.

Preparation of Consolidated Financial Statements

The federal government did not have adequate systems, controls, and procedures to properly prepare its consolidated financial statements. Specifically, we identified problems with compiling the consolidated financial statements, such as adequately ensuring that the information for each federal agency that was included in the consolidated financial statements was consistent with the underlying agency financial statements. In addition, we identified problems with the elimination of intragovernmental activity and balances. Later in this testimony, these matters are discussed further, along with certain corrective actions being taken. Also, disclosure of certain financial information was not presented in the consolidated financial statements in conformity with U.S. generally accepted accounting principles.

Ineffective Internal Control

In addition to the material deficiencies noted above, we found four other material weaknesses in internal control as of September 30, 2002: (1) several federal agencies continue to have significant deficiencies in the

[9]Trading partners are U.S. government agencies, departments, or other components included in the consolidated financial statements that do business with each other.

processes and procedures used to estimate the costs of their lending programs and value their loan receivables; (2) most federal agencies have not estimated or reported the magnitude of improper payments in their programs; (3) material internal control weaknesses and systems deficiencies continue to affect the federal government's ability to effectively manage its tax collection activities; and (4) federal agencies have not yet institutionalized comprehensive information security management programs.

Loans Receivable and Loan Guarantee Liabilities

Prior to fiscal year 2001, we cited accounting for loans receivable and loan guarantee liabilities as a material deficiency contributing to our disclaimer of opinion because certain key federal credit agencies could not reliably estimate the costs of their lending programs or determine the net loan amounts expected to be collected. In fiscal year 2001, due to significant improvements at USDA, we removed this area from the list of issues contributing to our disclaimer. Nevertheless, several federal agencies continue to have significant deficiencies in the processes and procedures used to estimate the costs of their lending programs and value their loan receivables.

In a recent report on SBA's loan asset sale program,[10] we reviewed SBA's budgeting and accounting for loan sales and found that SBA incorrectly calculated the accounting losses on the loan sales and lacked reliable financial data to determine the overall financial impact of the sales. Further, because SBA did not analyze the effect of loan sales on its remaining portfolio, its reestimates of loan program costs for the budget and financial statements may contain significant errors. In addition, SBA could not explain significant declines in its loss allowance account for disaster loans. SBA's inspector general and its independent auditor agreed with our findings, and the independent auditor withdrew its unqualified audit opinions on SBA's fiscal years 2001 and 2000 financial statements. Until SBA corrects these errors and determines the cause of the precipitous decline in the loss allowance account for disaster loans, SBA's financial statements cannot be relied upon. Further, the reliability of current and future subsidy cost estimates will remain unknown. These errors and the lack of key analyses also mean that congressional decision makers are not

[10]U.S. General Accounting Office, *Small Business Administration: Accounting Anomalies and Limited Operational Data Make Results of Loan Sales Uncertain*, GAO-03-87 (Washington, D.C.: Jan. 3, 2003).

receiving accurate financial data to make informed decisions about SBA's budget and the level of appropriations the agency should receive.

In addition, we again noted that certain other federal credit agencies continue to require significant adjustments to the estimates of program costs, net loan amounts to be collected, and related notes. Auditors for these agencies reported related material internal control weaknesses.

Improper Payments

Across the federal government, improper payments occur in a variety of programs and activities, including those related to health care, contract management, federal financial assistance, and tax refunds.[11] Many improper payments occur in federal programs that are administered by entities other than the federal government. In general, improper payments often result from a lack of or an inadequate system of internal controls. While estimates of improper payments disclosed in federal agency financial statements totaled approximately $20 billion for both fiscal years 2002 and 2001, the federal government did not estimate the full extent of improper payments. The President's Management Agenda includes addressing erroneous payments (a term we consider synonymous with improper payments) as one of the key elements for improving financial performance.

The Department of Health and Human Services (HHS) has been reporting a national estimate of improper Medicare fee-for-service payments as part of its annual financial statements since fiscal year 1996. In fiscal year 2002, HHS reported estimated improper Medicare fee-for-service payments of approximately $13.3 billion, or about 6.3 percent of such benefits. HHS's Centers for Medicare and Medicaid Services (CMS) has initiated projects to improve the precision of Medicare fee-for-service improper payment estimates and aid in the development of corrective actions to reduce improper payment losses. For example, CMS developed a comprehensive error-testing program that will produce contractor-, provider-, and benefit-specific error rates. These error rates can be aggregated to add greater precision to the national Medicare fee-for-service error rate estimates.

However, most federal agencies have not estimated or reported the magnitude of improper payments in their programs and comprehensively

[11] Improper payments include inadvertent errors, such as duplicate payments and miscalculations, payments for unsupported or inadequately supported claims, payments for services not rendered, payments to ineligible beneficiaries, and payments resulting from fraud and abuse by program participants and/or federal employees.

addressed this issue in their annual performance plans under the Government Performance and Results Act (GPRA) of 1993. For example, IRS follows up on only a portion of the suspicious Earned Income Tax Credit (EITC) claims it identifies, although the EITC has historically been vulnerable to high rates of invalid claims. In February 2002, IRS estimated that taxpayers filed returns for tax year 1999 claiming at least $8.5 billion in invalid EITCs, of which only $1.2 billion (14 percent) either was recovered or was expected to be recovered through compliance efforts. Although the full extent of refunds resulting from invalid EITCs is unknown, IRS has not routinely estimated the potential magnitude of invalid refunds and has not disclosed an annual estimate of improper payments in its financial reports. As a result, the amount of improper payments included in the almost $28 billion IRS disbursed for EITCs for fiscal year 2002 is unknown.

Without systematically measuring the extent of improper payments, federal agency management cannot determine (1) whether problems exist that merit agency action, (2) what mitigation strategies are appropriate and the amount to invest in them, and (3) whether efforts implemented to reduce improper payments are successful. OMB, which has shown leadership in this area, now requires annual submissions on improper payments from 15 federal agencies. Specifically, OMB requires actual and projected information on erroneous payment rates and the status of actions taken to reduce improper payments. Further, the Improper Payments Information Act of 2002[12] requires federal agencies to (1) annually review programs and activities that they administer to identify those that may be susceptible to significant improper payments, (2) estimate improper payments in susceptible programs and activities, and (3) provide reports to the Congress that include such information as the status of actions to reduce improper payments for programs and activities with estimated improper payments of $10 million or more.

Tax Collection Activities

Material internal control weaknesses and systems deficiencies continue to affect the federal government's ability to effectively manage its tax collection activities.[13] This situation continues to result in the need for extensive, costly, and time-consuming ad hoc programming and analyses, as well as material audit adjustments, to prepare basic financial

[12]Pub. L. No. 107-300, 116 Stat. 2350 (Nov. 26, 2002).

[13]U.S. General Accounting Office, *Financial Audit: IRS's Fiscal Years 2002 and 2001 Financial Statements*, GAO-03-243 (Washington, D.C.: Nov. 15, 2002).

information. As further discussed later in this testimony, this approach cannot be used to prepare such information on a timely, routine basis to assist in ongoing decision making. Additionally, the severity of the system deficiencies that give rise to the need to resort to such procedures for financial reporting purposes, as well as deficient physical safeguards, result in burden on taxpayers and lost revenue.

The lack of appropriate subsidiary systems to track the status of taxpayer accounts and material weaknesses in financial reporting affect the government's ability to make informed decisions about collection efforts. Due to errors and delays in recording activity in taxpayer accounts, taxpayers were not always being credited for payments made on their tax liabilities. In addition, the federal government did not always follow up on potential unreported or underreported taxes and did not always pursue collection efforts against taxpayers owing taxes to the federal government. This could result in billions of dollars not being collected and adversely affect future compliance.

The federal government continues to be vulnerable to lost tax revenue due to weaknesses in controls intended to maximize the government's ability to collect what is owed and to minimize the risk of payment of improper refunds. The federal government identifies billions of dollars of potentially underreported taxes and improper refunds each year. However, due in large part to perceived resource constraints, the federal government selects only a portion of the questionable cases it identifies for follow-up investigation and action. In addition, the federal government often does not initiate follow-up on the cases it selects until months after the related tax returns have been filed and any related refunds disbursed, affecting its chances of collecting amounts due on these cases. Consequently, the federal government is exposed to potentially significant losses from reduced revenue and disbursements of improper refunds. Finally, continued weaknesses in physical controls over cash, checks, and sensitive data received from taxpayers increase both the federal government's and the taxpayers' exposure to losses and increases the risk of taxpayers becoming victims of crimes committed through identity fraud.

IRS senior management continues to be committed to addressing many of these operational and financial management issues and has made a number of improvements to address some of these weaknesses. Successful implementation of long-term efforts to resolve these serious problems will require the continued commitment of IRS management as well as substantial resources and expertise.

Information Security Weaknesses

GAO has reported information security over computerized operations as a governmentwide high-risk area since February 1997.[14] Information security weaknesses are placing enormous amounts of federal government assets at risk of inadvertent or deliberate misuse, financial information at risk of unauthorized modification or destruction, sensitive information at risk of inappropriate disclosure, and critical operations at risk of disruption. The federal government is not in a position to estimate the full magnitude of actual damage and loss resulting from federal information security weaknesses because it is likely that many such incidents are either not detected or not reported. Although progress has been made, federal agencies have not yet institutionalized comprehensive security management programs, which are critical to resolving information security problems and managing information security risk on an ongoing basis.

The information security weaknesses continue to cover the full range of information security controls. For example, access controls were not effective in limiting or detecting inappropriate access to information resources, such as ensuring that only authorized individuals can read, alter, or delete data. In addition, software change controls were ineffective in ensuring that only properly authorized and tested software programs were implemented. Further, duties were not appropriately segregated to reduce the risk that one individual could conduct unauthorized transactions without being detected. Finally, sensitive operating system software was not adequately controlled, and adequate steps had not been taken to ensure continuity of operations.

[14] U.S. General Accounting Office, *High-Risk Series: An Update*, GAO-03-119 (Washington, D.C.: January 2003).

Through the recently enacted Federal Information Security Management Act of 2002 (FISMA),[15] the Congress has continued its efforts to improve federal information security by permanently authorizing and strengthening the information security program, evaluation, and reporting requirements established by federal government information security reform legislation.[16] This information security reform legislation has been a significant step in improving federal agencies' information security programs and addressing their serious, pervasive information security weaknesses, and, among other benefits, has increased management attention to and accountability for information security. FISMA will further strengthen federal information security by requiring the National Institute of Standards and Technology to develop mandatory minimum information security requirements.

The administration has also taken actions to improve information security. For example, OMB created an annual reporting process that includes federal agency preparation of corrective action plans to track progress in correcting identified weaknesses. Further, in February 2003, the President issued the *National Strategy to Secure Cyberspace*, which sets national priorities for reducing threats from and vulnerabilities to cyberattacks and improving the nation's response to cyberincidents.

Providing Sustained Leadership and Oversight for Effective Implementation of Financial Management Reform

Over the past year, the JFMIP Principals continued our efforts, begun in August 2001, to accelerate progress in financial management reform. This involved our personal commitment to provide the leadership necessary to address pressing governmentwide financial management issues. Also, President Bush has implemented the President's Management Agenda to provide direction to, and to closely monitor, management reform across government, which encompasses improved financial performance. Actions such as these are important elements of ensuring the government's full and effective implementation of the federal financial management reforms enacted by the Congress.

[15]Pub. L. No. 107-347, Title III, 116 Stat. 2946 (Dec. 17, 2002).

[16]Floyd D. Spence National Defense Authorization Act for Fiscal Year 2001, Pub. L. No. 106-398, Title X, Subtitle G, 114 Stat. 1654A-266 (Oct. 30, 2000).

The JFMIP Principals' Initiative

Since August 2001, the JFMIP Principals have established an excellent working relationship, a basis for action, and a sense of urgency through which significant and meaningful progress can be achieved. In fiscal year 2002, JFMIP Principals continued the series of regular, deliberative meetings that focused on key financial management reform issues such as

- defining success measures for financial management performance that go far beyond an unqualified audit opinion on financial statements and include measures such as financial management systems that routinely provide timely, reliable, and useful financial information and no material internal control weaknesses or material noncompliance with laws and regulations and Federal Financial Management Improvement Act of 1996 (FFMIA) requirements;[17]
- restructuring the Federal Accounting Standards Advisory Board's (FASAB) composition to enhance the independence of the Board and increase public involvement in setting standards for federal financial accounting and reporting;
- significantly accelerating financial statement reporting to improve timeliness for decision making and to discourage costly efforts designed to obtain unqualified opinions on financial statements without addressing underlying systems challenges;
- establishing audit advisory committees for selected major federal agencies; and
- addressing difficult accounting and reporting issues, including impediments to an audit opinion on the U.S. government's consolidated financial statements and reporting updated social insurance financial information in the U.S. government's consolidated financial statements.

Continued personal involvement of the JFMIP Principals is critical to the full and successful implementation of federal financial management reform and to providing greater transparency and accountability in managing

[17]FFMIA requires auditors, as part of CFO Act agencies' financial statement audits, to report whether agencies' financial management systems substantially comply with (1) federal financial management systems requirements, (2) applicable federal accounting standards (U.S. generally accepted accounting principles), and (3) the federal government's SGL at the transaction level.

federal programs and financial resources. At the end of fiscal year 2002, I ended my 2-year term as Chair of the JFMIP Principals, and the Chair rotated to Office of Management and Budget Director Daniels. I look forward to working with the new Chair, Treasury Secretary Snow, and Office of Personnel Management Director James in the upcoming months to continue this important dialogue and build on the strong working relationships that we have established.

The President's Management Agenda

President Bush has established an agenda for improving the management and performance of the federal government that targets the most apparent deficiencies where the opportunity to improve performance is the greatest. It is no accident that the President's Management Agenda has a strong correlation to GAO's high-risk list. This is just one example of how GAO and OMB have worked constructively to identify key issues deserving increased attention throughout government. As stated in the President's Management Agenda—and we wholeheartedly agree—there are few items more urgent than ensuring that the federal government is well run and results-oriented.

The President's Management Agenda, which is a starting point for management reform, includes improved financial management performance as one of the five governmentwide management goals. Other governmentwide initiatives of the President's Management Agenda include strategic management of human capital, competitive sourcing, expanded electronic government, and budget and performance integration.

In particular, the improved financial management performance initiative is aimed at ensuring that federal financial systems produce accurate and timely information to support operating, budget, and policy decisions. Also, this initiative focuses special attention on addressing erroneous payments, credit card abuse in the federal government, and asset management, areas for which we have reported problems and challenges.[18]

[18]U.S. General Accounting Office, *Financial Management: Coordinated Approach Needed to Address the Government's Improper Payments Problems*, GAO-02-749 (Washington, D.C.: Aug. 9, 2002); *Government Purchase Cards: Control Weaknesses Expose Agencies to Fraud and Abuse*, GAO-02-676T (Washington, D.C.: May 1, 2002); *High-Risk Series: Federal Real Property*, GAO-03-122 (Washington, D.C.: January 2003).

Under the improved financial management performance initiative, agencies are expected to improve the timeliness, enhance the usefulness, and ensure the reliability of financial information. The expected result is integrated financial and performance management systems that routinely produce information that is (1) timely, to measure and effect performance immediately, (2) useful, to make more informed operational and investing decisions, and (3) reliable, to ensure consistent and comparable trend analysis over time and to facilitate better performance measurement and decision making. This result is a key to successfully achieving the goals set out by the Congress in the CFO Act and other federal financial management reform legislation.

Central to effectively addressing the federal government's management problems and providing a solid base for successful transformation efforts is recognition that the five governmentwide initiatives cannot be addressed in an isolated or piecemeal fashion from other major management challenges and high risks facing federal agencies. Rather, these efforts are mutually reinforcing and must be addressed in an integrated way to ensure that they drive a broader transformation of the cultures of federal agencies.

The Executive Branch Management Scorecard

The administration is using the Executive Branch Management Scorecard to highlight federal agencies' progress in achieving management and performance improvements embodied in the President's Management Agenda. The Executive Branch Management Scorecard grades selected federal agencies' performance regarding the five governmentwide initiatives by using broad standards and a red-yellow-green coding system to indicate the level at which agencies are meeting the standards.

In the financial management area, while recognizing the importance of achieving an unqualified opinion from auditors on financial statements, the scorecard focuses on the fundamental and systemic issues that must be addressed in order to generate timely, accurate, and useful financial information. The scorecard also measures whether agencies have any material internal control weaknesses or material noncompliances with laws and regulations, and whether agencies meet FFMIA requirements. The December 31, 2002, scorecard's results show dramatically the extent of work remaining across government to improve financial and other management areas. For financial performance, most of the selected federal agencies were scored in the red category. This is not surprising, considering the well-recognized need to transform financial management and other business processes at federal agencies such as DOD, the results of our analyses under FFMIA, and the various financial management operations we have designated as high risk.[19] Some of the selected agencies improved their scores from the initial baseline evaluation as of September 30, 2001; however, other agencies' scores declined, reflecting increased challenges.

The focus that the administration's scorecard approach brings to improving management and performance, including financial management performance, is certainly a step in the right direction. The value of the scorecard is not in the scoring per se, but in the degree to which scores lead to sustained focus and demonstrable improvements. This will depend on continued efforts to assess progress and maintain accountability to ensure that agencies are able to, in fact, improve their performance. It will be important that there be continuous rigor in the scoring process in order for this approach to be credible and effective in providing the proper incentives that produce lasting results. Also, it is important to recognize that many of the challenges the federal government faces, such as improving financial management, are long-standing and complex, and will require sustained attention.

[19]As reported in GAO-03-119, we have identified financial management as a high-risk area at DOD, Treasury's IRS, USDA's Forest Service, and the Department of Transportation's Federal Aviation Administration.

Building on the Success of Unqualified Audit Opinions

Building on the success that has been achieved in obtaining unqualified audit opinions, federal agency management must continue to work toward fully resolving the pervasive and generally long-standing material weaknesses that have been reported for the past 6 fiscal years. The underlying causes of these issues are significant financial management systems weaknesses, problems with fundamental recordkeeping and financial reporting, incomplete documentation, and weak internal control. In identifying improved financial management performance as one of its five governmentwide initiatives, the President's Management Agenda stated that a clean (unqualified) financial audit opinion is a basic prescription for any well-managed organization. It recognized that "most federal agencies that obtain clean audits only do so after making extraordinary, labor-intensive assaults on financial records." Further, the President's Management Agenda stated that without sound internal control and accurate and timely financial information, it is not possible to accomplish the President's agenda to secure the best performance and highest measure of accountability for the American people.

Irrespective of the unqualified opinions on their financial statements, many federal agencies do not have timely, accurate, and useful financial information and sound controls with which to make informed decisions and to ensure accountability on an ongoing basis. While federal agencies have continued to make progress in obtaining unqualified audit opinions on annual financial statements, many of these opinions were obtained by expending significant resources on extensive ad hoc procedures and making billions of dollars in adjustments to derive the financial statements months after the end of a fiscal year. Several examples follow. The need for such resource-intensive procedures primarily results from inadequate financial management systems.

- After receiving a disclaimer of opinion for fiscal year 2001, NASA was able to produce auditable financial statements for fiscal year 2002; however, the auditors reported that significant weaknesses still existed in NASA's internal controls related to accounting for the International Space Station and for equipment and materials held by contractors. Because of these control weaknesses, the auditors found numerous errors in property records and had to significantly expand the scope of their testing. To correct auditor-identified errors, NASA had to make about $11 billion of adjustments to its records. The auditors also identified a material weakness related to NASA's process for preparing its financial statements and performance and accountability report.

Deficiencies included errors made in recording significant adjustments to the statements and reports. Auditors attributed the errors to insufficient resources to address the volume of work needed to compile the financial statements, lack of an integrated financial management system, lack of understanding by NASA staff of new federal reporting requirements, and lack of quality controls over financial reporting.

- After 8 consecutive years of disclaimers of opinion, USDA received an unqualified opinion on its fiscal year 2002 financial statements. While we consider this a positive step toward achieving financial accountability, it took extraordinary efforts outside the normal business processes by the department and its auditors, particularly at the Forest Service. The USDA Office of Inspector General's transmittal letter for the fiscal year 2002 Forest Service audit report stated that "the Forest Service does not yet operate as an effective, sustainable, and accountable financial management organization. The fiscal year 2002 ending account balances were primarily derived from a 2-year audit effort on beginning balances and numerous statistical samples of fiscal year 2002 transactions. As a result of these efforts, multiple adjustments were processed to the general ledger and/or subsidiary ledgers. For example, the financial statement line item General Property, Plant and Equipment, Net, was reduced by over $1 billion based on audit coverage. The achievement of an unqualified opinion, therefore, did not necessarily result from improvement in underlying financial management systems, but rather as an extensive ad hoc effort." If USDA is to achieve and sustain financial accountability, it must fundamentally improve its underlying internal controls, financial management systems, and operations to allow for the routine production of accurate, relevant, and timely data to support program management.

- Our unqualified opinions on IRS's fiscal years 2002 and 2001 financial statements were made possible by the extraordinary efforts of IRS senior management and staff to develop processes to compensate for serious internal control and systems deficiencies. As noted earlier in this testimony, IRS made significant progress during fiscal year 2002. Nonetheless, it continued to require costly, resource-intensive processes; statistical projections; external contractors; substantial adjustments; and monumental human efforts to derive reliable year-end balances for its financial statements. For example, IRS still does not have a detailed record, or subsidiary ledger, for taxes receivable to allow it to track and manage amounts due from taxpayers. To enable it to report a reliable taxes receivable balance in the absence of a subsidiary ledger, IRS has, for the last 6 years, relied on a complex statistical sampling approach that requires substantial human and financial resources to conduct, takes months to complete, and yields tens of billions of dollars of adjustments. Similarly, while progress has been made, IRS does not have an integrated property management system that appropriately records property and equipment additions and disposals as they occur and links costs on the accounting records to the property records.

It will be increasingly difficult for federal agencies to continue to rely on significant costly and time-intensive manual efforts to achieve or maintain unqualified opinions until automated, integrated processes and systems are implemented that readily produce the necessary information. As a result, many federal agencies must accelerate their efforts to improve underlying financial management systems and controls, which is consistent with reaching the financial management success measures envisioned by the JFMIP Principals and called for by the President's Management Agenda.

FFMIA requires auditors, as part of CFO Act agencies' financial statement audits, to report whether agencies' financial management systems substantially comply with (1) federal financial management systems requirements, (2) applicable federal accounting standards (U.S. generally accepted accounting principles), and (3) the federal government's Standard General Ledger (SGL) at the transaction level. For fiscal year 2002, auditors for 19 CFO Act agencies reported that the agencies' financial management systems did not comply substantially with one or more of these three FFMIA requirements. For the remaining 5 CFO Act agencies, auditors provided negative assurance, meaning that nothing came to their attention indicating that these agencies' financial management systems did not substantially meet FFMIA requirements. The auditors for these 5 agencies did not definitively state whether these agencies' systems substantially complied with FFMIA requirements, as is required under the statute. Meeting the requirements of FFMIA has presented long-standing, significant challenges. These challenges will be resolved only through time, investment, and sustained emphasis on correcting deficiencies in federal financial management systems. GAO plans to report to the Congress by October 1, 2003, on CFO Act agencies' FFMIA implementation for fiscal year 2002, as required by the act.

While federal agencies continue to make progress in addressing weaknesses in their financial management systems, the serious shortcomings reported for these systems result in the lack of reliable financial information needed for making operating decisions day to day, managing the federal government's operations more efficiently and effectively, measuring program performance, executing the budget, maintaining accountability, and preparing financial statements.

For example, federal agency financial management systems are required to produce information on the full cost of programs and projects. This is not a new expectation—the requirement for managerial cost information has been in place for more than a decade, since 1990 under the CFO Act and since 1998 stemming from applicable accounting standards. Currently, some federal agencies are only able to provide cost accounting information at the end of the fiscal year through periodic cost surveys. Some federal agencies, such as the Department of the Interior's Bureau of Land Management, are experimenting with methods of accumulating and assigning costs to obtain the managerial cost information needed to enhance programs, improve processes, establish fees, develop budgets, prepare financial reports, and report on performance. Having such financial information is the goal of FFMIA and the CFO Act, necessary for implementing GPRA, and critical to the transition to a more results-oriented federal government as envisioned in the President's Management Agenda.

To remedy financial management systems weaknesses and carry out the President's Management Agenda for improving financial management, OMB, and the CFO Act agencies will need to aggressively and rigorously collaborate. Our work to identify financial management best practices in world-class organizations[20] has identified key factors for successfully modernizing financial systems, including (1) reengineering business processes in conjunction with implementing new technology, (2) developing systems that support the partnership between finance and operations, and (3) translating financial data into meaningful data. We identified other financial management best practices as well, such as (1) providing clear, strong executive leadership, (2) making financial management an entitywide priority, and (3) building a culture of control and accountability.

The size and complexity of many federal agencies and the discipline needed to overhaul or replace their financial management systems present

[20]U.S. General Accounting Office, *Executive Guide: Creating Value Through World-class Financial Management*, GAO/AIMD-00-134 (Washington, D.C.: April 2000).

a significant challenge—not simply a challenge to overcome a technical glitch, but a demanding management challenge that requires attention from the highest levels of the federal government along with sufficient human capital resources to effect lasting change. This will be a particular challenge at the new Department of Homeland Security (DHS), where federal agencies, many of which have ongoing challenges in their systems, processes, or internal controls over financial information, are becoming part of the new department. DHS, along with other federal agencies, has a stewardship obligation to prevent fraud, waste, and abuse, to use tax dollars appropriately, and to ensure financial accountability to the President, the Congress, and the American people. In addition to addressing incoming agencies' challenges, DHS will need to focus on building future systems as part of its enterprise architecture approach to ensure an overarching framework for the agency's integrated financial management processes. Plans must be developed and implemented to bridge the many financial environments in which incoming agencies currently operate to an integrated DHS system.

We recognize that it will take time, investment, and sustained emphasis on correcting deficiencies to improve federal financial management systems at DHS and other federal agencies to the level required by FFMIA. The JFMIP Principals' leadership, commitment, and oversight will be important to provide the needed impetus to meet this challenge.

Addressing Major Impediments to an Opinion on Consolidated Financial Statements

As I mentioned earlier, for the past 6 fiscal years, the federal government has been required to prepare, and have audited, consolidated financial statements. Successfully meeting this requirement is tightly linked to the requirement for the 24 CFO Act agencies to also have audited financial statements. This has stimulated extensive cooperative efforts and considerable attention by agency chief financial officers, inspectors general, Treasury and OMB officials, and GAO. With the benefit of several years' experience by the federal government in having the required financial statements subjected to audit, the time has come to focus even more intensified attention on the most serious obstacles to achieving an opinion on the U.S. government's consolidated financial statements. In this regard, the JFMIP Principals have discussed plans and strategies for addressing impediments to an opinion on the U.S. government's consolidated financial statements. Three major impediments to an opinion on the consolidated financial statements are (1) serious financial management problems at DOD, (2) the federal government's inability to fully account for and reconcile billions of dollars of transactions between federal entities, and (3) the federal government's inability to properly prepare the consolidated financial statements.

Reforming Financial Management at DOD

Essential to achieving an opinion on the consolidated financial statements is resolution of the serious financial management problems at DOD, which we have designated as high risk since 1995. In accordance with provisions of the National Defense Authorization Act for fiscal year 2002,[21] DOD reported that the department's financial management systems were not able to provide adequate evidence supporting material amounts in its fiscal year 2002 financial statements. DOD asserted that it is unable to comply with applicable financial reporting requirements for (1) property, plant, and equipment, (2) inventory and operating materials and supplies, (3) military retirement health care actuarial liability, (4) environmental liabilities, (5) intragovernmental eliminations and related accounting adjustments, and (6) cost accounting by suborganization/responsibility segment and major program. Based largely on DOD's assertion, the DOD inspector general again disclaimed an opinion on DOD's financial statements for fiscal year 2002 as it had for the previous 6 fiscal years.

To date, none of the military services or major DOD components has passed the test of an independent financial audit because of pervasive weaknesses in DOD's financial management systems, operations, and internal control, including an inability to compile financial statements that comply with generally accepted accounting principles. The department has made progress in a number of areas but is far from solving a range of serious financial management problems. Their resolution, however, is key to having auditable consolidated financial statements because DOD had budget authority of $385 billion for fiscal year 2002, or about 18 percent of the entire federal budget; is accountable for a vast amount of government assets worldwide; and incurs a substantial amount of the reported liabilities.

[21]Section 1008 of the National Defense Authorization Act for fiscal year 2002, Pub. L. No. 107-107, 115 Stat. 1012 (Dec. 28, 2001), provides a framework for redirecting the department's resources from the preparation and audit of financial statements to improvement of DOD's financial management systems and financial management policies, procedures, and internal controls. Under this legislation, the department will also be required to report to the Congress on how resources have been redirected and the progress that has been achieved.

DOD's financial management deficiencies adversely affect not only the department's ability to prepare auditable financial statements, but also its ability to control costs, ensure basic accountability, anticipate future costs and claims on the budget (such as for health care, weapons systems, and environmental liabilities), measure performance, maintain control of funds, prevent fraud, and address pressing management issues. For example, we recently reported on fundamental flaws in DOD's systems, processes, and overall internal control environment, such as those related to

- pervasive purchase and travel card breakdowns that resulted in numerous instances of potentially fraudulent, improper, and abusive transactions and increased DOD's vulnerability to theft and misuse of government property;
- adjustments to DOD's closed appropriations that resulted in about $615 million in adjustments that should not have been made, including $146 million that were illegal; and
- accountability over critical items, such as chemical and biological protective garments, that resulted in DOD's excessing and selling unused garment sets for about $3 each, while simultaneously procuring hundreds of thousands of similar garment sets for over $200 per set.

As discussed in our recent reporting[22] on the management challenges facing the government, overhauling DOD's financial management operations represents a major challenge that goes far beyond financial accounting to the very fiber of the department's range of business operations and management culture. In prior years, DOD expended significant resources and made material amounts of adjustments to derive its financial statements. However, such statements were determined to be unauditable. In this regard, as previously mentioned, section 1008 of the National Defense Authorization Act for fiscal year 2002 provides a framework for redirecting the department's resources from the preparation and audit of financial statements to improving DOD's financial management systems and financial management policies, procedures, and internal controls. Administrations over the past 12 years have attempted to address these problems in various ways but have largely been unsuccessful despite good intentions and significant effort.

[22]U.S. General Accounting Office, *Major Management Challenges and Program Risks: Department of Defense*, GAO-03-98 (Washington, D.C.: January 2003).

As we testified in March 2002 and highlighted in our more recent reports, four underlying causes of problems have impeded past reform efforts at DOD:

- The lack of accountability and sustained top-level leadership hinders DOD's ability to meet its performance goals. Major improvement initiatives must have the direct, active support and involvement of the Secretary and Deputy Secretary of Defense to ensure that daily activities throughout the department remain focused on achieving shared, agencywide outcomes and success. Furthermore, sustaining commitment by top leadership to performance goals is a particular challenge for DOD because the average tenure of DOD's top political appointees is only 1.7 years. Based on our survey of best practices of world-class financial management organizations, it is clear that strong executive leadership is essential to (1) making financial management an entitywide priority, (2) redefining the role of finance, (3) providing meaningful information to decision makers, and (4) building a team of people that delivers results.
- Cultural resistance to change and stovepiped operations have impeded DOD's ability to implement broad-based management reforms. We found that the effectiveness of the Defense Management Council, established in 1997, was impaired because members were not able to put aside their particular military services' or DOD agencies' interests to focus on departmentwide approaches. DOD's stovepiped approach is most evident in its current financial management systems environment, which DOD recently estimated to include 1,800 systems and system development projects—many of which were developed in piecemeal fashion and evolved to accommodate different organizations, each with its own policies and procedures.
- Lack of clear, linked goals and performance measures impedes DOD's ability to attain strategic goals with the risk that units are operating autonomously, rather than collectively. In our assessment of DOD's fiscal year 2000 Financial Management Improvement Plan—its most recent plan—we found that it presented the military services' and DOD components' individual improvement initiatives but did not clearly articulate how their individual efforts would result in a collective, integrated DOD-wide approach to financial management improvement. In addition, the plan did not include performance measures to assess DOD's progress in resolving

financial management problems. Furthermore, while DOD plans to invest billions of dollars in modernizing its financial management systems, it is in the initial stages of developing an overall blueprint, or enterprise architecture, to guide and direct these investments.

- Lack of incentives to change existing "business-as-usual" processes, systems, and structures contributes to DOD's inability to carry out needed fundamental reform. Traditionally, DOD has focused more on justifying its need for more funding and moving programs and operations through the process than on achieving better program outcomes. It does not (1) reward behaviors that contribute to DOD-wide and congressional goals, (2) develop motivational incentives for decision makers to guide them toward better program outcomes, or (3) provide congressional focus on more results-oriented and resource allocation decisions.

On September 10, 2001, Secretary of Defense Rumsfeld recognized the far-reaching nature of DOD's financial management problems and announced a broad, top-priority initiative intended to "transform the way the department works and what it works on." This new broad-based business transformation initiative, led by DOD's Senior Executive Council and the Business Initiative Council, incorporates a number of defense reform initiatives begun under previous administrations but also encompasses additional fundamental business reform proposals. In announcing his initiative, Secretary Rumsfeld recognized that transformation would be difficult and expected the needed changes would take 8 or more years to complete. The Secretary's initiative is consistent with the findings of an independent study he commissioned that concluded that DOD would have to undergo "a radical financial management transformation" and that it would take more than a decade to achieve. Secretary Rumsfeld recently included improving DOD's financial management as one of his top 10 priorities, and DOD has already taken a number of actions intended to address its serious financial management problems. In addition, as I previously mentioned, DOD has a major effort under way to develop a DOD enterprise architecture that is intended to prescribe a blueprint for operational and technological changes in its financial and related business systems operations. While DOD has a long way to go, its efforts over the past year represent important progress. The level of top leadership that has been brought to bear on this challenge will have to be sustained with a goal of achieving lasting improvement that truly transforms DOD's business systems and operations and enables the department to meet the mandate of the CFO Act and achieve the President's Management Agenda's goal of improved financial management performance.

Addressing Intragovernmental Transactions

OMB and Treasury require CFO Act agencies to reconcile selected intragovernmental activity and balances with their "trading partners" and to report on the extent and results of intragovernmental activity and balances reconciliation efforts. The inspectors general reviewed these reports and communicated the results of their reviews to OMB, Treasury, and GAO. A substantial number of the CFO Act agencies did not fully perform the required reconciliations for fiscal years 2002 and 2001, citing reasons such as (1) trading partners not providing needed data, (2) limitations and incompatibility of agency and trading partner systems, and (3) human resource issues. For both of these years, amounts reported for federal agency trading partners for certain intragovernmental accounts were significantly out of balance. In addition, significant differences in other intragovernmental accounts, primarily related to appropriations, will need to be resolved.

As we reported last year, the heart of the intragovernmental transactions issue is that the federal government lacked clearly articulated business rules for these transactions so that they would be handled consistently by agencies. To address certain issues that contributed to the out of balance condition for intragovernmental activity and balances, OMB has established a set of standard business rules for governmentwide transactions among trading partners and is requiring quarterly reconciliations of intragovernmental activity and balances beginning in fiscal year 2003. For example, in accordance with one of the business rules, beginning in fiscal year 2003 for intragovernmental investments with Treasury's Bureau of the Public Debt (BPD), BPD and trading partner agencies are required to use the same method for recording amortization on market-based notes, bonds, and zero coupon securities. In the past, differences in the amortization methods being used have caused out of balance conditions for related intragovernmental activity and balances. Resolving the intragovernmental transactions problem remains a difficult challenge and will require a commitment by the CFO Act agencies and continued strong leadership by OMB.

Preparing the Consolidated Financial Statements

The federal government did not have adequate systems, controls, and procedures to properly prepare its consolidated financial statements, as described below. Also, disclosure of certain financial information was not presented in the consolidated financial statements in conformity with U.S. generally accepted accounting principles.

Consolidated Financial Statement Compilation

Due to the current financial statement compilation process, the federal government could not adequately ensure that the information for each federal agency included in the consolidated financial statements was consistent with the underlying agency financial statements. This process also requires significant human and financial resources and does not adequately leverage the existing work and work products resulting from federal agencies' audited financial statements. The problems are further compounded by the need for broad changes in the structure of the government's SGL accounts and the process for maintaining the SGL.

The net position reported in the consolidated financial statements is derived by subtracting liabilities from assets, rather than through balanced accounting entries. To make the fiscal years 2002 and 2001 consolidated financial statements balance, Treasury recorded a net $17.1 billion and $17.3 billion decrease to net operating cost, respectively, on the Statement of Operations and Changes in Net Position, which it labeled unreconciled transactions. An additional net $12.5 billion and $3.9 billion of unreconciled transactions were improperly recorded in net cost for fiscal years 2002 and 2001, respectively. Treasury attributes these net unreconciled transaction amounts primarily to the federal government's inability to properly identify and eliminate transactions between governmental entities, federal agency adjustments that affected net position, and other errors. Treasury was unable to adequately identify and explain the gross components of such amounts. Unreconciled transactions also may exist because the federal government does not have effective controls over reconciling net position.

The federal government did not have an adequate process to reconcile the operating results, which for fiscal year 2002 showed a net operating cost of $364.9 billion, to the budget results, which for the same period showed a unified budget deficit of $157.7 billion.[23]

[23]Statement of Federal Financial Accounting Standards No. 24, *Selected Standards for the Consolidated Financial Report of the United States Government*, issued January 2003, requires the federal government to provide a financial statement that reconciles net operating revenue (or cost) and the annual unified budget surplus (or deficit).

Treasury is currently developing a new system and procedures to prepare the consolidated financial statements beginning with fiscal year 2004. These actions are intended to, among other things, directly link information from federal agencies' audited financial statements to amounts reported in the consolidated financial statements and facilitate the reconciliation of net position. Resolving the consolidated financial statement compilation process issues will require continued strong leadership by Treasury management.

Elimination of Intragovernmental Activity and Balances from the Consolidated Financial Statements

Consolidated financial statements are intended to present the results of operations and financial position of the components that make up a reporting entity as if the entity were a single enterprise. When preparing the consolidated financial statements, the preparer must eliminate intragovernmental activity and balances between the federal agencies. Because of federal agencies' problems in handling their intragovernmental transactions, Treasury's ability to eliminate these transactions is impaired. Significant differences reported in intragovernmental accounts, as noted above, have been identified. To help federal agencies better perform their reconciliations, Treasury recently began providing agencies with detailed trading partner information. Intragovernmental activity and balances are "dropped" or "offset" in the preparation of the consolidated financial statements rather than eliminated through balanced accounting entries. This contributes to the federal government's inability to determine the impact of these differences on amounts reported in the consolidated financial statements. The continued strong leadership of Treasury will be important to resolving the issues surrounding the elimination of intragovernmental activity and balances from the consolidated financial statements.

Protecting the Public Interest

Two audit matters have come to the fore and are key to protecting the public interest. One matter involves auditors' responsibilities for reporting on internal control, and the other concerns auditor independence.

Auditors' Responsibilities for Reporting on Internal Control

We have long believed that auditors have an important responsibility to provide an opinion on the effectiveness of internal control over financial reporting and compliance with laws and regulations. Currently, this is not required by American Institute of Certified Public Accountants (AICPA) auditing standards or by OMB in its guidance[24] to auditors conducting federal agency financial statement audits.

For financial statements audits that we conduct—which include the U.S. government's consolidated financial statements, the financial statements of the IRS, the Schedules of Federal Debt managed by the Bureau of the Public Debt, and the financial statements of the Federal Deposit Insurance Corporation Funds and numerous small entities' operations and funds—we issue a separate opinion on the effectiveness of internal control over financial reporting and compliance with laws and regulations.

For years we have provided opinions on internal control effectiveness because of the importance of internal control to protecting the public's interest. Our reports have engendered major improvements in internal control. As you might expect, as part of the annual audit of our own financial statements, we practice what we recommend to others and contract with an independent public accounting firm for both an opinion on our financial statements and an opinion on the effectiveness of our internal control over financial reporting and compliance with laws and regulations.

Although OMB requires testing of these internal controls, auditors are not required to provide an opinion on internal control effectiveness. However, we found that 3 of the 24 CFO Act agency auditors (those for the General Services Administration, SSA, and the Nuclear Regulatory Commission) provided an opinion on the effectiveness of internal control as of September 30, 2002. Our hope is that all CFO Act agencies and the new DHS will follow suit in future years. In this regard, last year, in response to major breakdowns in corporate accountability, auditing, and corporate governance in the private sector, the Congress passed the Sarbanes-Oxley Act of 2002[25] to, among other things, improve quality and transparency in financial reporting and independent audits of publicly traded companies ("issuers"). In the area of internal control reporting, issuers are required to

[24]Office of Management and Budget, *Audit Requirements for Federal Financial Statements*, Bulletin 01-02 (Washington, D.C.: Oct. 19, 2000).

[25]Sarbanes-Oxley Act of 2002, Pub. L. No. 107-204, 116 Stat. 745 (July 30, 2002).

establish and maintain adequate internal control structure and procedures for financial reporting and include in the annual report a statement of management's responsibility for and management's assessment of the effectiveness of those controls and procedures. In addition, an issuer's auditor is required to attest to, and report on, the assessment made by the management of the issuer on the effectiveness of internal control over financial reporting. In other words, an issuer's auditor will provide an attestation, or opinion, on management's assertions about the effectiveness of internal controls over financial reporting.

"Internal controls and procedures for financial reporting" is generally defined as controls that pertain to the preparation of external financial statements that are fairly presented in conformity with generally accepted accounting principles. Specifically, controls over financial reporting include the objectives of ensuring that transactions are properly recorded, processed, and summarized to permit the preparation of financial statements in conformity generally accepted accounting principles.

GAO strongly believes that auditor reporting on internal control is a critical component of monitoring the effectiveness of an organization's internal control and accountability. By giving assurance about internal control, auditors of federal financial statements can better serve their clients and other financial statements users and better protect the public interest by having a greater role in providing assurances of the effectiveness of internal control in deterring fraudulent financial reporting, protecting assets, and providing an early warning of internal control weaknesses.

Auditor Independence and Government Auditing Standards

The independence of auditors—both in fact and appearance—is critical to the credibility of financial reporting. Auditors have the capability of performing a range of valuable services for their clients, and providing certain nonaudit services can ultimately be beneficial to federal entities. However, in some circumstances, it is not appropriate for auditors to perform both audit and certain nonaudit services for the same client. In these circumstances, the auditor, the client, or both will have to make a choice as to which of these services the auditor will provide.

These concepts, which I continue to strongly believe are in the public interest, were reflected in the revisions to auditor independence requirements for government audits,[26] which GAO issued last year as part of *Government Auditing Standards*.[27] The standard, among other things, strengthens the rules associated with providing nonaudit services and includes a principle-based approach to addressing this issue, supplemented with certain safeguards. The two overarching principles in the standard for nonaudit services are that

- auditors should not perform management functions or make management decisions, and
- auditors should not audit their own work or provide nonaudit services in situations where the amounts or services involved are significant or material to the subject matter of the audit.

In making judgments on independence under *Government Auditing Standards* and applying the independence standard's principles and safeguards, audit organizations should take a "substance over form" approach and consider the nature and significance of the services provided to the audited entity—the facts and circumstances. Before an audit organization agrees to perform nonaudit services, it should carefully consider the need to avoid situations that could lead reasonable third parties with knowledge of the facts and circumstances to conclude that the auditor is not able to maintain independence in conducting audits. It is imperative that auditors always be viewed as independent in fact and appearance.

[26] U.S. General Accounting Office, *Government Auditing Standards, Amendment No. 3, Independence*, GAO-02-388G (Washington, D.C.: January 2002).

[27] *Government Auditing Standards* was first published in 1972 and is commonly referred to as the "Yellow Book." It covers federal entities and organizations that receive federal funds. Various laws require compliance with the standards in connection with audits of federal entities and funds. Further, many states and local governments and other entities, both domestically and internationally, have voluntarily adopted these standards.

Understandably, GAO received many inquiries about the new independence standard due to its significant effect on auditors in connection with audits of those who are required to use or have adopted the use of *Government Auditing Standards.* Working with the Comptroller General's Advisory Council on Government Auditing Standards[28] and other interested parties, we issued further guidance in the form of questions and answers related to the independence standard's implementation time frame, underlying concepts, and application in specific nonaudit circumstances.[29]

The independence standard and the recently issued question and answer document are the initial steps in GAO's continuing efforts to enhance *Government Auditing Standards* and educate auditors on revisions to these standards and on implementation issues surrounding the independence standard. Within the next several months, GAO will issue revisions to *Government Auditing Standards* to help ensure that the standards continue to meet the needs of the audit community and the public it serves. The revision will expand and change (1) the types of audits and services that can be performed under the standards and (2) the application of the standards, where relevant, to be consistent with the various types of audits. Changes are also being made to enhance the understandability of the standards. To educate the audit community about the revised standards as well as the independence standard, GAO continues to provide many presentations to government auditors and private practitioners, in addition to answering hundreds of questions regarding implementation issues.

Closing Comments

Our report on the U.S. government's consolidated financial statements for fiscal years 2002 and 2001 highlights the need to continue addressing the government's serious financial management weaknesses. Looking beyond current progress by federal agencies in attaining unqualified opinions on financial statements, it will be essential for the federal government to begin moving away from the extraordinary efforts many federal agencies continue to use to prepare financial statements and toward giving

[28]The Advisory Council includes 21 experts in financial and performance auditing and reporting—drawn from all levels of government, academia, private enterprise, and public accounting—who advise the Comptroller General on *Government Auditing Standards.*

[29]U.S. General Accounting Office, *Government Auditing Standards, Answers to Independence Standard Questions,* GAO-02-870G (Washington, D.C.: July 2002).

prominence to strengthening the government's financial systems, reporting, and controls. This approach becomes even more critical as the federal government progresses to an accelerated financial statement reporting time frame, and it is the only way the government can meet the end goal of making timely, accurate, and useful financial information routinely available to the Congress, other policymakers, and the American public.

The requirement for timely, accurate, and useful financial and performance management information is greater than ever, as the Congress and the administration prepare to meet tomorrow's fiscal challenges. This type of financial information is central to managing the federal government's operations more efficiently, effectively, and economically and in supporting GPRA. Moreover, meaningful financial and performance information can form the basis for reconsidering the relevance or "fit" of any federal program or activity in today's world and for the future.

In closing Mr. Chairman, I want to underscore the importance of the additional impetus provided by President Bush through his President's Management Agenda and the Executive Branch Management Scorecard for coming to grips with federal financial management problems, indeed management problems across the board. Regarding DOD in particular, Secretary of Defense Rumsfeld's vision and approach for transforming the department's full range of business processes is serious and encouraging. These efforts will be key to fulfilling the President's Management Agenda and addressing the largest obstacle to an opinion on the U.S. government's consolidated financial statements. The cooperative efforts spearheaded by the JFMIP Principals have been most encouraging in developing the short- and long-term strategies and plans necessary to address many of the problems I have discussed this morning. In addition, GAO has probably never had a better working relationship with OMB and cabinet level and other key officials on a range of "good government issues" that are of critical importance and are inherently non-partisan in nature. While these and other factors provide an enhanced likelihood for success, in the end it is results that count.

Finally, I want to reiterate the value of sustained congressional interest in these issues, as demonstrated by this hearing and those the former Subcommittee on Government Efficiency, Financial Management, and Intergovernmental Relations held over the past several years to oversee financial management reform. It will also be key that the appropriations, budget, authorizing, and oversight committees hold agency top leadership accountable for resolving these problems and that they support improvement efforts.

Contacts

For further information regarding this testimony, please contact Jeffrey C. Steinhoff, Managing Director, and Gary T. Engel, Director, Financial Management and Assurance, at (202) 512-2600.

Appendix I

CFO Act Agencies: Fiscal Year 2002 Audit Results, Principal Auditors, and Number of Other Audit Contractors

24 CFO Act agencies	Audit results	Principal auditor	Number of other audit contractors
Agency for International Development	Qualified[a]	Inspector General	1
Agriculture	Unqualified	Inspector General	2
Commerce	Unqualified	KPMG LLP	1
Defense	Disclaimer	Inspector General	1
Education	Unqualified	Ernst & Young LLP	0
Energy	Unqualified	KPMG LLP	4
Environmental Protection Agency	Unqualified	Inspector General	0
Federal Emergency Management Agency	Unqualified	KPMG LLP	0
General Services Administration	Unqualified	PricewaterhouseCoopers LLP	0
Health and Human Services	Unqualified	Inspector General	4
Housing and Urban Development	Unqualified	Inspector General	1
Interior	Unqualified	KPMG LLP	0
Justice	Unqualified	PricewaterhouseCoopers LLP	2
Labor	Unqualified	Inspector General	5
National Aeronautics and Space Administration	Unqualified	PricewaterhouseCoopers LLP	1
National Science Foundation	Unqualified	KPMG LLP	0
Nuclear Regulatory Commission	Unqualified	R. Navarro & Associates, Inc.	0
Office of Personnel Management	Unqualified	KPMG LLP	0
Small Business Administration	Disclaimer	Cotton & Company LLP	0
Social Security Administration	Unqualified	PricewaterhouseCoopers LLP	0
State	Unqualified	Leonard G. Birnbaum and Company, LLP	0
Transportation	Unqualified	Inspector General	2
Treasury	Unqualified	Inspector General	6[b]
Veterans Affairs	Unqualified	Deloitte & Touche LLP	0

[a]Qualified for the Statement of Net Cost; unqualified for all other statements.

[b]In addition, GAO audited the Internal Revenue Service's financial statements and the Schedules of Federal Debt Managed by the Bureau of the Public Debt.

GAO
Accountability * Integrity * Reliability

24 CFO Act Agencies: Fiscal Year 2002 Audit Results Reported by Auditors

24 CFO Act agencies	Audit results	No material weaknesses	No reported noncompliances with laws and regulations[2]	No nonsubstantial compliance with FFMIA requirements[3]
Agency for International Development	Qualified[1]			
Agriculture	Unqualified			
Commerce	Unqualified			
Defense	Disclaimer			
Education	Unqualified		✓	
Energy	Unqualified	✓	✓	✓
Environmental Protection Agency	Unqualified	✓		✓
Federal Emergency Management Agency	Unqualified			
General Services Administration	Unqualified	✓	✓	✓
Health and Human Services	Unqualified		✓	
Housing and Urban Development	Unqualified		✓	
Interior	Unqualified			
Justice	Unqualified		✓	
Labor	Unqualified	✓	✓	
National Aeronautics and Space Administration	Unqualified		✓	
National Science Foundation	Unqualified	✓	✓	✓
Nuclear Regulatory Commission	Unqualified			
Office of Personnel Management	Unqualified	✓	✓	
Small Business Administration	Disclaimer			
Social Security Administration	Unqualified	✓	✓	✓
State	Unqualified			
Transportation	Unqualified			
Treasury	Unqualified			
Veterans Affairs	Unqualified		✓	
		7	12	5

[1] Qualified for the Statement of Net Cost; unqualified for all other statements.
[2] Does not include auditors' determination of agencies' substantial compliance with FFMIA requirements.
[3] Auditors provided negative assurance, meaning that nothing came to their attention indicating that these agencies' financial management systems did not substantially meet FFMIA requirements.

Selected Fiscal Exposures: Sources and Example
(End of Fiscal Year 2002)

Type	**Example** (dollars in billions)
Explicit liabilities	• Publicly held debt ($3,540) • Military & civilian pension & post-retirement health ($2,673) • Veterans benefits payable ($849) • Environmental and disposal liabilities ($273) • Loan guarantees ($28)
Explicit financial commitments	• Undelivered orders ($539) • Long-term leases ($50)
Explicit financial contingencies	• Unadjudicated claims ($9) • National insurance programs ($43)
Implicit exposures implied by current policies or the public's expectations about the role of government	• Debt held by government accounts ($2,674) • Future Social Security benefit payments ($3,549)* • Future Medicare Part A benefit payments ($5,931)* • Life cycle costs including deferred &future maintenance and operating costs (amount unknown)

Source: GAO.

*These amounts represent NPV over 75 years and are net of debt held by the Trust Funds ($1,378 billion for Social Security and $235 billion for Medicare Part A). Figures for Social security and Medicare Part A are as of January 1, 2003.

Composition of Spending as a Share of GDP
Assuming Discretionary Spending Grows with GDP after 2003 and the 2001 Tax Cuts Do Not Sunset

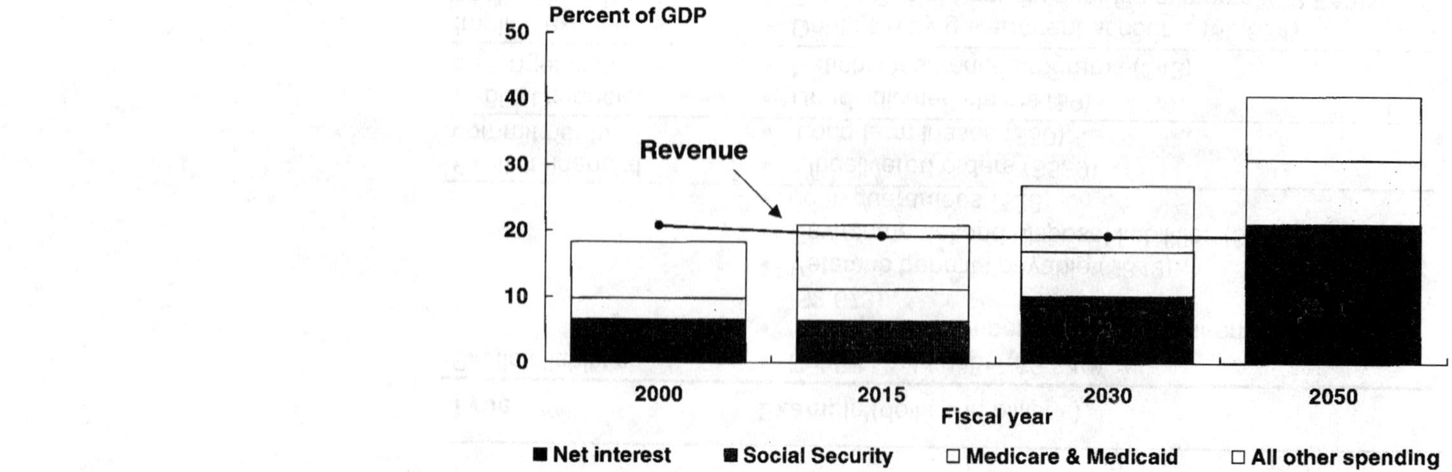

Source: GAO's March 2003 analysis.

Note: Assumes currently scheduled Social Security benefits are paid in full throughout the simulation period.

Fiscal Year 2002 CFO Act Agency Results Reported by Auditors

Agencies with clean opinions	Agencies with clean opinions and no material weaknesses or noncompliances
21[a]	**4**[b]

[a]Agriculture, Commerce, Education, Energy, Federal Emergency Management Agency, Health and Human Services, Housing and Urban Development, Interior, Justice, Labor, State, Transportation, Treasury, Veterans Affairs, Environmental Protection Agency, General Services Administration, National Aeronautics and Space Administration, National Science Foundation, Nuclear Regulatory Commission, Office of Personnel Management, and Social Security Administration.

[b]Energy, General Services Administration, National Science Foundation, and Social Security Administration.

Source: GAO

Mr. PLATTS. Thank you, Mr. Walker for your testimony and your very frank assessment of where we are from a management sense and why we need to do a lot better as we move to the years to come and the challenges we are going to face. Also, your comments regarding former Chairman Steve Horn and his efforts are very appropriate. I am honored to succeed Chairman Horn in this position.

Ms. Springer.

Ms. SPRINGER. Thank you, Mr. Chairman.

I am honored to testify for the first time as the Controller, Office of Management and Budget before this subcommittee. I feel today as I have many times before reporting to the audit committee of corporate boards of directors. As I did in those meetings, I am here to provide you with a response by management to the issues presented in the auditor's report on the Federal Government's consolidated financial statements for the fiscal years ended September 30, 2002 and 2001.

The General Accounting Office has issued a disclaimer of opinion on the consolidated financial statements for these periods as Mr. Walker has noted. In so doing, material weaknesses were noted in the following areas: (1) the area of assets, property, plant, and equipment and inventories and related property; (2) the area of liabilities, and commitments and contingencies; (3) cost of government operations and disbursement activity; (4) accounting for and reconciliation of intragovernmental activity and balances; and (5) preparation of consolidated financial statements. The primary source of weakness in the first three areas is the Department of Defense. Items four and five are process impediments that have governmentwide impact.

GAO also identified the following material weaknesses in internal control throughout the executive branch: (1) loans receivable and loan guarantee liabilities; (2) improper payments; (3) information security; and (4) tax collection activities. OMB agrees with GAO that these are areas of weakness. We are not satisfied with this result. In fact, we believe that even unqualified audit opinions and the absence of material weaknesses do not necessarily indicate the presence of first class financial management. First class financial management requires integration of the financial impact of agency decisions and activities in operational execution and senior management decisionmaking. These things would be accompanied by accountability standard setting, performance tracking and other analyses. These are among the characteristics we should seek in government every bit as much as they are expected in the private sector. These are the objectives of the Improved Financial Performance Initiative which the President's Management Agenda is focused on.

The administration is making a concerted effort to address the weaknesses identified by GAO and agency Inspectors General and independent auditors. For example, we are working to identify the root causes and current status of, as well as action plans to remedy, the deficiencies at the Department of Defense. Some of these actions will be near term. Others will take longer and will be dependent on the new financial management systems implementation. OMB has reviewed with DOD its assessment and plans for each area identified by GAO. Our most recent update was just last week when I met with not only Comptroller Zakheim but also with the Inspector General. These meetings are typical of planning sessions we have with every CFO Act agency's CFO and their IG. These meetings will be an ongoing series and at those we will be reviewing plans to review how to achieve clean audits and also remove other material weaknesses, and meeting accelerated reporting deadlines. As you know, our reporting deadline in 2004 has been accelerated to November 15 with the governmentwide report coming out 1 month later in December.

In our judgment, DOD is identifying its problems and is engaged in both short and long term remediation activities. These activities would substantially address the first three material weaknesses I noted previously. OMB will continue to monitor this progress with both the department and its IG.

Regarding intragovernmental transactions, we have new rules in place that govern the manner in which agencies record intragovernmental transactions. Simply put, these rules once and for all standardize the governmentwide processing and recording of intragovernmental activity. In conjunction with the automated process by which we will compile the governmentwide financial statements in the near future, will go a long way toward resolving the other material weaknesses that contribute to the disclaimer of opinion by the auditors.

As you have heard at the recent testimony on the President's Management Agenda, notable progress was made in fiscal year 2002 in agency financial reporting. For 2002, a record number of the government's major departments and agencies received unqualified opinions on their annual audited financial statements, 21 of 24 up from 18 in fiscal year 2001. I appreciate Mr. Walker going back even farther than that to six to show even further progress over the years.

Two agencies, Treasury and the Social Security Administration, met the new governmentwide standard for timeliness of reliable financial information 2 years early, the November 15 deadline. All agencies for 2003 have targeted earlier dates required to make a step forward, about half of them looking to meet the November date in 2003.

In addition to DOD, only the Small Business Administration and the U.S. Agency for International Development are keeping us from our goal of unqualified audit opinions on the financial statements of the major departments and agencies. I met with the DOD Comptroller just last week to assess the department's status. I am also meeting with officials from USAID and SBA in the coming weeks to begin regular updates on their progress in getting clean audit opinions. I want to note for the subcommittee that USAID received an unqualified opinion for four of its five financial statements and a qualified opinion on the fifth statement. The fifth statement is the statement of net costs and there are still some remaining material weaknesses with which we concur with GAO. There are plans in place to remediate the weaknesses on that statement. I should mention this is up from three statements that were unqualified and two disclaimed in the previous year.

Part of the President's Improved Financial Performance Initiative is our effort to reduce erroneous payments. While GAO in the past had tallied just $20 billion in erroneous payments, OMB reported to the Congress last year that our effort, which requires erroneous payment estimates for major benefit programs has raised that total estimate to $35 billion annually. We are expanding our efforts in this area with the implementation of the Improper Payments Information Act of 2002, which originated in this subcommittee. This act requires an estimate of the extent of erroneous payments from all Federal programs. Program-wide erroneous payment estimates can only help stem the loss to the Federal Government in waste, fraud, and abuse, too much of which is taking place without accounting.

Our erroneous payment efforts are not just about estimates. The President's fiscal year 2004 budget includes a $100 million increase to clarify Earned Income Tax Credit rules and to help ensure only eligible taxpayers receive payments. This investment could help us reduce the more than $9 billion in erroneous EITC payments we make annually. The administration has also proposed a number of tools to give agencies the ability to further save us billions of dollars over time.

Mr. Chairman, I would be derelict not to mention one of the great challenges before us, the migration of the component agencies to the new Department of Homeland Security which will pose a major challenge from a financial management perspective. Disparate systems at different stages of implementation are just one of the complicating factors that will be dealt with by the new department. We plan and are working closely with Under Secretary Hale and her staff in meeting these challenges.

Our auditor, GAO, has highlighted many of our weaknesses, but I don't want to pass up the opportunity to highlight some of the favorable assertions made in GAO's report about the efforts the Bush administration is making to improve financial management throughout the government. "Across government, financial management improvement initiatives are under way that, if effectively implemented, have the potential to appreciably improve the quality of the Federal Government's financial management and reporting. A number of Federal agencies have started to make progress in their efforts to modernize their financial management systems and improve financial management performance as called for in the President's Management Agenda. The President's Management Agenda includes improved financial performance as one of the top five governmentwide management goals. This is a step in the right direction to improving management and performance.

The attention we are paying to improving financial performance and the progress we have made thus far move us down the playing field, but still short of the goal line. It is important that we not lose sight of these achievements, however. Even though no score appears on the board until we have crossed the line, we have moved inside the red zone and the goal is in sight. This administration is committed, with the help of this subcommittee, to achieving the first class financial management of which we and the American people can be proud.

Thank you, Mr. Chairman.

[The prepared statement of Ms. Springer follows:]

Testimony of
The Honorable Linda M. Springer
Controller, Office of Federal Financial Management
Office of Management and Budget
before the
Subcommittee on Government Efficiency and Financial Management
Committee on Government Reform
United States House of Representatives
April 8, 2003

Thank you, Mr. Chairman.

I am honored to testify for the first time as the Controller at the Office of Management and Budget (OMB) before this subcommittee. I feel today as I have many times before reporting to the Audit Committee of corporate Boards of Directors. As I did in those meetings, I am here to provide you with a response by management to the issues presented in the auditor's report on the Federal Government's consolidated financial statements for the fiscal years ended September 30, 2002 and 2001.

The General Accounting Office (GAO) has issued a disclaimer of opinion on the consolidated financial statements for these periods. In so doing, material weaknesses were noted in the following areas:

1. Assets: Property, Plant, and Equipment and Inventories and Related Property
2. Liabilities: Liabilities and Commitments and Contingencies
3. Cost of Government Operations and Disbursement Activity
4. Accounting for and Reconciliation of Intragovernmental Activity and Balances; and
5. Preparation of Consolidated Financial Statements.

The primary source of weakness in the first three areas is the Department of Defense. Items 4 and 5 are process impediments that have government-wide impact.

GAO also identified the following material weaknesses in internal control throughout the Executive Branch:

1. Loans Receivable and Loan Guarantee Liabilities
2. Improper Payments
3. Information Security; and
4. Tax Collection Activities.

OMB agrees with GAO that these are areas of weakness. We are not satisfied with this result. In fact, we believe that even unqualified audit opinions and the absence of material weaknesses do not necessarily indicate the presence of first class financial management. First class financial management requires integration of the financial impact of agency activities in operational execution and senior management decision making, accompanied by accountability standard setting, performance tracking and other analyses. These are among the characteristics we should seek in government every bit as much as they are expected in the private sector. And these are the objectives of the Improved Financial Performance Initiative of the President's Management Agenda.

The Administration is making a concerted effort to address the weaknesses identified by GAO and agency Inspectors General and independent auditors. For example, we are working to identify the root causes and current status of, as well as action plans to remedy, the deficiencies at the Department of Defense (DOD). Some of these actions will be near term. Others will take longer and will be dependent on the new financial management systems implementation. OMB has reviewed with DOD its assessment and plans for each area identified by GAO. Our most recent update was just last week at planning sessions we have initiated with every CFO Act agency's CFO and IG. These meetings are the first of what will be an ongoing review of plans to meet the financial reporting objectives of achieving unqualified audit opinions, eliminating material weaknesses, and meeting accelerated reporting deadlines.

In our judgment, DOD is identifying its problems and is engaged in both short and long term remediation activities. This should substantially address the first three material weaknesses. OMB will continue to monitor this progress with both the department and its IG.

Regarding intragovernmental transactions, we have new rules in place that govern the manner in which agencies record intragovernmental transactions. Simply put, these rules once and for all standardize the government-wide processing and recording of intragovernmental activity. This, in conjunction with the automated process by which we will compile the government-wide financial statements in the near future, will go a long way toward resolution of the other material weaknesses that contribute to the disclaimer of opinion by the auditors.

As you have heard at the recent testimony on the President's Management Agenda, notable progress was made in Fiscal Year 2002 in agency financial reporting. This year a record number of the government's major departments and agencies received unqualified opinions on their annual audited financial statements – 21 of 24 – up from 18 in Fiscal Year 2001. Two agencies – Treasury and the Social Security Administration – met the new government-wide standard for timeliness of reliable financial information two years early. In addition to DOD, only the Small Business Administration (SBA) and the U.S. Agency for International Development (USAID) are keeping us from our goal of unqualified audit opinions on the financial statements of the major departments and agencies. I met with the DOD Comptroller just last week to assess the department's status. I am meeting with officials from USAID on April 16th and SBA on May 1st to begin regular updates on their progress in both getting a clean audit opinion and meeting the President's accelerated financial reporting deadline. I want to note for the subcommittee that USAID received an unqualified opinion for 4 of its 5 principal financial statements and a qualified opinion on the fifth statement.

Part of the President's Improved Financial Performance Initiative is our effort to reduce erroneous payments. While GAO in the past had tallied just $20 billion in erroneous payments, OMB reported to the Congress last year that our effort, which requires erroneous payment estimates for major benefit programs that make payments in excess of $1.2 trillion annually, has raised the total estimate of erroneous payments to $35 billion annually. We are expanding our efforts in this area with the implementation of the Improper Payments Information Act of 2002, which originated in this subcommittee. This act requires an estimate of the extent of erroneous payments from *all* federal programs. Program-wide erroneous payment estimates can only help stem the loss to the federal government in waste, fraud, and abuse—too much of which is taking place without an accounting. But our erroneous payment efforts are not just about estimates. The President's FY 2004 budget includes a $100 million increase to clarify Earned Income Tax Credit (EITC) rules and to help ensure only eligible taxpayers receive payments. This investment could help us reduce the more than $9 billion in erroneous EITC payments we make annually. The Administration has also proposed a number of common sense proposals to give agencies tools they can use to verify the eligibility of applicants for Student Financial Assistance, housing subsidies, and unemployment insurance. These provisions, if enacted, could save us billions of dollars over time.

Of course, Mr. Chairman, I would be derelict not to mention one of the great challenges before us. The migration of the component agencies to the new Department of Homeland Security will present a major challenge from a financial management perspective. Disparate systems at different stages of implementation is just one of many complicating issues that the new Department presents. I plan to work closely with Under Secretary Hale to meet these challenges.

Our auditor, GAO, has highlighted many of our weaknesses. I will not pass up the opportunity to highlight some of the favorable assertions made in GAO's report about the efforts the Bush Administration is making to improve financial management throughout the government.

> *Across government, financial management improvement initiatives are under way that, if effectively implemented, have the potential to appreciably improve the*

> *quality of the federal government's financial management and reporting. A number of federal agencies have started to make progress in their efforts to modernize their financial management systems and improve financial management performance as called for in the President's Management Agenda.*
>
> *[T]he President's Management Agenda includes improved financial performance as one of the top five governmentwide management goals . . . This is a step in the right direction to improving management and performance.*

The attention we are paying to improving financial performance and the progress we have made thus far move us down the playing field, but still short of the goal line. It is important that we not lose sight of these achievements, however. Even though no score appears on the board until we've crossed the line, we have moved inside the red zone and the goal is in sight. This administration is committed, with the help of this subcommittee, to achieving the first class financial management of which we and the American people can be proud.

Mr. PLATTS. Thank you, Ms. Springer, for your substantive statement. We commend you for having already met with the DOD Comptroller and having SBA and USAID meetings scheduled to get your arms around the challenges in those agencies. We look forward to working with you.

Ms. SPRINGER. Thank you.

Mr. PLATTS. Mr. Hammond.

Mr. HAMMOND. Thank you, Mr. Chairman and members of the subcommittee.

Thank you for the opportunity to discuss the Financial Report of the U.S. Government. I would ask that the Chairman include the full text of my statement in the record but on behalf of the Secretary, I would like to thank you for focusing on and promoting the improvement of Federal Government financial accountability and reporting. We appreciate the subcommittee's continued leadership in this area.

Before I continue, I wish to congratulate you, Chairman Platts, on your appointment to chair this important panel. We had the pleasure of working very closely with Chairman Horn in previous Congresses and look forward to the same effective working relationship with your subcommittee.

The financial report is prepared pursuant to the Government Management Reform Act of 1994 to provide the President, the Congress and the American people with reliable financial information on an accrual basis about the Federal Government's operations. The Federal Government does not have a single bottom line that reflects its financial status. Therefore the information included in the financial report provides a comprehensive view of the Federal Government's finances that is not available elsewhere. The report covers all accounts from the executive branch but since the legislative and judicial branches are not required to prepare financial statements, recording information included from those branches is limited.

The Department of the Treasury is committed to producing accurate and useful governmentwide financial statements and continues to devote considerable resources at both the departmental level and at the Financial Management Service to making the government's finances as clear and transparent as possible. Everyone should be able to understand the cost of government operations and the implications of its commitments. The financial report is important in this respect because it highlights the difference between budget and accrual-based reporting. Accrual results offer a longer term view that extends the horizon for making budget decisions. This year, for the first time, we have grouped together all of the significant liabilities, stewardship responsibilities and other commitments in the front of the report, specifically on page 6. They total an estimated $31.1 trillion, almost 10 times the size of the debt held by the public. These amounts reported separately for several years become more transparent we believe when they are presented together for analysis.

The importance of this report is also highlighted in this year's results. For fiscal 2002, the Financial Report indicates an accrual-based net operating cost for the Federal Government of $365 billion. This compares to the more familiar $158 billion budget deficit reported last fall. The principal difference between these two figures is the accrual recognition of an additional over $157 billion of veterans benefit costs and liabilities. Without accrual-based reporting, these differences would be lost and would not be visible to the American taxpayer.

For Treasury to achieve its goals for improved financial reporting, continued strong support from OMB and all the Chief Financial Officers Act agencies will be critical. We have charted a course for continued improvements and we expect to implement them fully in the fiscal 2004 statements.

In my remaining time, Mr. Chairman, I will discuss our progress over the last year and outline some of the planned improvements.

As noted, this is the 6th year we have prepared consolidated, governmentwide financial reports. Each year there have been significant improvements in the agency data. This year, 21 of the 24 CFO Act agencies received clean audit opinions, up from 6 agencies only 7 years ago. Also, three major agencies, the Social Security Administration, Treasury Department and yes, the U.S. Postal Service, completed their financial statement audits by November 15, 3½ months earlier than statutorily required for the first two and the Postal Service has no due date on their financial statements that I am aware of.

Data for the Financial Report primarily comes from the 24 CFO Act agencies, 9 other significant entities such as the Postal Service and 180 smaller entities. Preparing the report, as you can imagine, is a complex task based on a foundation of over 2,000 individual reporting components' standardized Standard General Ledger reporting, highlighting the importance of good data quality. In other words, the data has to be right the first time coming from the agency level. There is really very little opportunity to massage it at the end.

In auditing the Financial Report, GAO was unable to express an opinion on the reliability of this year's financial statements, primarily due to three areas: data and financial system problems at the Department of Defense, preparation issues relating to intragovernmental balances both in agency data quality and consolidation eliminations, and consistency with agency financial reporting. However, GAO did acknowledge in its audit report that financial management improvement initiatives are being undertaken that will improve the quality of financial management and reporting in the Federal Government. These include DOD improving its financial management and related systems, Treasury and OMB taking a number of steps to address the intragovernmental issues and development of a new preparation process for the financial report itself. The above indicates that the current state of Federal financial reporting needs improvement.

I am confident that a creative and committed effort by top management at Treasury, program agencies, OMB, the CFO Council, and GAO can result in breakthrough changes. Later this year, for example, Treasury will provide agencies with a detailed account statement monthly to help them reconcile their fund balance with Treasury. The production of this account statement is the next step in a Web-based, governmentwide accounting modernization project that, when completed, will provide agencies with better tools for both reporting their financial information and monitoring its status. This new approach will enable agencies to eliminate duplicative reporting and costly, manually intensive reconciliations.

After extensive consultation with our auditors and financial managers throughout the government, it was clear that broad and sweeping changes in the compilation process of the Financial Report were necessary to address the "process" related material weaknesses. Treasury, in coordination with OMB, is adopting a new process to collect agency financial information that will be used to prepare the fiscal 2004 Financial Report. Agencies will follow an automated process to convert their audited financial statements to a standardized statement format which will ensure the data in the report is consistent with the data in the agency's audited financial statements. These changes, along with modifications in the manner in which we perform eliminations and consolidate the data, should eliminate the material compilation weaknesses identified by GAO.

We are also in the process of accelerating agency budget reporting. To facilitate the accelerated deadlines for submission of annual agency-level financial statements and the governmentwide financial statements, Treasury's Financial Management Service has accelerated the monthly agency budget reporting timeframes. The accelerated timeframes will support agencies accelerated preparation of their year-end audited financial statements and provide for more timely information to improve decisionmaking.

Treasury is the first to acknowledge that reporting financial results 6 months after the close of a fiscal year is simply not good enough. Accordingly, the scheduled date for issuing the fiscal 2004 financial report is December 15, 2004. Meeting this timeframe is dependent on agencies meeting their accelerated reporting dates. I currently chair the CFO council committee charged with assisting agencies in meeting the accelerated issuance dates for fiscal 2004 and believe these dates are in fact achievable. This is a significant step forward since we will finally have actual data about the prior year for use in the budget deliberations for the coming year and managers throughout government will have accurate data for day-to-day decisionmaking at all levels.

A core responsibility of the Treasury Department is to accurately and effectively report on the Nation's finances. Long ago we accomplished transparency of budget results. Our challenge is to bring that same transparency to the full extent of our financial operations. We have made great progress in that quest, and the Federal financial community working together will soon realize that vision.

Thank you again for the opportunity to testify and I would be happy to answer any questions the committee may have.

[The prepared statement of Mr. Hammond follows:]

STATEMENT OF DONALD V. HAMMOND
Fiscal Assistant Secretary
U.S. Department of the Treasury
before the
SUBCOMMITTEE ON GOVERNMENT EFFICIENCY AND FINANCIAL MANAGEMENT
COMMITTEE ON GOVERNMENT REFORM
UNITED STATES HOUSE OF REPRESENTATIVES
April 8, 2003

FINANCIAL REPORT OF THE UNITED STATES GOVERNMENT FISCAL YEAR 2002

Mr. Chairman and Members of the Subcommittee,

Thank you for the opportunity to discuss the *Financial Report of the United States Government* (Financial Report). On behalf of the Secretary, I would like to thank you for focusing on and promoting the improvement of Federal Government financial accountability and reporting. These are important transitional times, and we appreciate your leadership on these issues. Before I continue, I wish to congratulate you, Chairman Platts, on your appointment to chair this important panel. We had the pleasure of working very closely with Chairman Horn in previous Congresses on improving government financial management, and we look forward to the same effective working relationship with your Subcommittee in the months and years ahead.

As you know, the Government Management Reform Act of 1994 requires that not later than March 31 of each year, the Secretary of the Treasury, in coordination with the Office of Management and Budget (OMB) Director, shall prepare and submit to the President and the Congress financial statements subject to audit for the preceding fiscal year. They are prepared in accordance with generally accepted accounting principles as established by the Federal Accounting Standards Advisory Board (FASAB).

The Financial Report is prepared in order to provide the President, the Congress, and the American people with reliable information about the financial position of the Federal Government on an accrual basis, the net cost of its operations, and the financing sources used to fund these operations. The Federal Government does not have a single bottom line that reflects its financial status, but the information included in the statements provides a comprehensive view of the Federal Government's finances that is not available elsewhere. The Financial Report consists of management's discussion and analysis, statements of net cost, statements of operations and changes in net position, reconciliations of net operating revenue (or cost) and unified budget surplus (or deficit), statements of changes in cash balance from unified budget and other activities, balance sheets, notes to the principal statements, and other useful information. The Financial Report covers all accounts from the executive branch. Since the legislative and judicial branches are not required to prepare financial statements, some limited reporting information from those branches is included.

IMPORTANCE OF THE FINANCIAL REPORT

The Department of the Treasury is committed to producing accurate and useful government-wide financial statements and continues to devote considerable resources to this effort. This report continues our efforts to fulfill our responsibilities to the Congress and the public by making the government's finances as clear and transparent as possible. Everyone should be able to understand the cost of the government's operations and the implications of its commitments. The Financial Report, which is prepared using the accrual basis of accounting, is intended to meet this objective. Under the accrual basis, transactions are reported when the events giving rise to the transactions occur rather than when cash is received or paid (cash basis).

The importance of this accrual-based report should not be overlooked. The changes affecting the Government over the past decade have resulted in a much smaller share of the budget that is discretionary. Almost two-thirds of the budget goes for mandatory spending such as Social Security and Medicare. Accrual results offer a longer-term view that extends the horizon for making budget decisions. The ability to assess the budget impact of policy decisions is enhanced when this analysis is used in conjunction with our traditional receipts and outlays information. The Financial Report is important in this respect because it highlights this difference, particularly in the Management's Discussion and Analysis section, which goes beyond simply reporting accounting results by discussing the effects of governmental commitments. This year, for the first time, we have grouped together all of the significant liabilities, stewardship responsibilities and other commitments in the front of the report. They total an estimated $31.1 trillion and represent a measure of the significant commitments the government has made. These amounts have been included separately in the report for several years; however, we believe they become more transparent when they are presented together.

The Financial Report is the only source of this financial information on a government-wide consolidated level, which provides a more transparent picture of the Government's financial position and operations. The importance of this report is also highlighted in this year's results. For fiscal 2002, the Financial Report indicates an accrual-based net operating cost of $365 billion. This compares to the $158 billion budget deficit, based generally on the cash basis, for this year's results. The principal difference is the accrual recognition of over $157 billion of veterans benefit costs. The Financial Report covers the disposition of more than $1.9 trillion in revenues and $2.3 trillion in operating costs, as well as extensive stewardship responsibilities and social insurance commitments, such as Social Security, Medicare, and liabilities including civilian and military retirement pensions and benefits.

For Treasury to achieve its goals for improved financial reporting, continued strong support from OMB and all the Chief Financial Officers Act agencies will be critical. We have charted a course for continued improvements, and we expect to implement the plan fully in the fiscal 2004 statements. In my remaining time, Mr. Chairman, I will discuss our progress in the last year and outline some of the planned improvements.

PROGRESS MADE THIS YEAR

This is the sixth year we have prepared consolidated, government-wide financial reports. There have been significant improvements in the agency data. This year, 21 of the 24 CFO Act agencies received clean audit opinions, up from 18 last year and just 6 agencies only 7 years ago. Also, three major agencies, the Social Security Administration, Treasury Department and U.S. Postal Service, completed their financial statement audits by November 15, which was three and a half months earlier than statutorily required. This is a significant achievement and is a model for all agencies to improve the timeliness and usefulness of their financial data. In addition to these improvements in timeliness and data quality, the report includes the summary schedule of total government commitments that improves the transparency of the data.

Data for the Financial Report primarily comes from 24 CFO Act agencies, nine other significant entities and 180 smaller entities. Each agency is financially independent and maintains its own financial system. Preparing the report is a complex task based on a foundation of over 2,000 individual reporting components' standardized Standard General Ledger reporting.

In auditing the Financial Report, GAO was unable to express an opinion on the reliability of this year's financial statements. This is due primarily to only three areas, data and financial system problems at the Department of Defense (DoD), preparation issues relating to intragovernmental balances both in agency data quality and consolidation eliminations, and consistency with agency financial reporting. However, GAO did acknowledge in its audit report that financial management improvement initiatives are being undertaken that will improve the quality of financial management and reporting in the Federal Government. For example, DoD has been aggressive in improving its financial management and has made real progress in rationalizing and streamlining its systems. In addition, Treasury and OMB have taken a number of steps to address the intragovernmental issue. OMB has issued new intragovernmental business rules for standardizing inter-agency transactions, which will help correct this situation in future years. Also, Treasury's Financial Management Service (FMS) developed a database tool to support Treasury analysis and agency reconciliation of trading partner differences. Finally, consistency will be assured with the identification of a new preparation process I will speak to shortly.

IMPROVEMENTS UNDERWAY

The current state of federal financial reporting needs improvement. I am confident that a creative and committed effort by top management at Treasury, program agencies, OMB, the CFO Council, and GAO can result in breakthrough changes. We are taking aggressive actions to improve government-wide financial management. Later this year, for example, Treasury will provide agencies with a detailed account statement to help them reconcile their fund balance with Treasury. For the very first time, agencies will have more timely access to this statement, as opposed to having to wait up to 45 days for a hard copy report to be issued. The production of this account statement is the next step in a government-wide accounting modernization project that, when completed, will provide agencies with better tools for both reporting their financial information and monitoring its status.

Next year, the plan is to continue the improvement to our systems by beginning to provide agencies the capability to capture and classify transactions directly to the appropriate account at the initiation of the transaction. When fully operational, agencies will have access to financial information in 1-2 days compared to the current timeframe of 15-18 days after the close of the month. This new approach will enable agencies to eliminate duplicative reporting and costly, manually intensive reconciliations.

After extensive consultation with financial managers throughout the government, it was clear that broad and sweeping changes in the compilation process of the Financial Report were necessary to address the "process" material weaknesses (i.e., significantly inadequate systems, controls, and procedures to prepare the Financial Report) identified by GAO. This will require a major rebuilding of the electronic processes used by Treasury's Financial Management Service to prepare the Financial Report.

Treasury, in coordination with OMB, is adopting a new process to collect agency financial information that will be used to prepare the fiscal 2004 Financial Report. The new data submission, referred to as the "closing package", will be a web-based submission. Agencies will follow an automated process to convert their audited financial statements to a standardized statement format. Using agency financial statement information in the preparation of the Financial Report will ensure that the data in the Financial Report is consistent with the data in agencies' audited financial statements. Having consistent data will better leverage audit work done at the agency level and allow GAO to rely on the agency-level audits. These changes, along with modifications in the manner in which FMS performs eliminations and consolidates the data, should eliminate the material compilation weaknesses identified by GAO.

We are also in the process of accelerating agency budget reporting. To facilitate the accelerated deadlines for submission of annual agency-level financial statements and the government-wide financial statements, FMS has accelerated the monthly agency budget reporting timeframes. Federal agencies are required to submit the monthly reporting data within three days following the close of the previous month. The accelerated monthly timeframes will provide the necessary discipline for agencies to prepare their year-end audited financial statements and provide for more timely information to improve decision-making.

The scheduled date for issuing the fiscal 2004 Financial Report is December 15, 2004. Meeting this accelerated timeframe is dependent on agencies improving the quality and timeliness of the information they report and the audit community responding to increased audit responsibilities. While the report was again issued on time, Treasury is the first to acknowledge that reporting financial results six months after the close of a fiscal year is simply not good enough. I currently chair the CFO council committee charged with assisting agencies in meeting the accelerated issuance dates required by OMB for fiscal 2004 for both agency-level financial statements and government-wide financial statements by identifying and removing barriers. This is a significant step forward since we will finally have actual data about the prior year for use in the budget deliberations for the coming year and managers throughout government will have accurate data for day-to-day decision making at all levels.

CONCLUSION

A core responsibility of the Treasury Department is to accurately and effectively report on the nation's finances. Providing transparency to government financial results has been a top priority starting with our first Treasury Secretary, Alexander Hamilton. Long ago we accomplished transparency of budget results.

Our challenge is to bring that same transparency to the full extent of our financial operations. We have made great progress in that quest, and the federal financial community working together will soon realize that vision.

Thank you, Mr. Chairman. This concludes my formal remarks and I would be happy to respond to questions.

Mr. PLATTS. Thank you, Mr. Hammond. I appreciate your testimony, as with each of the witnesses and the in-depth presentations and your shared efforts and interest in truly getting us to where the American taxpayer knows how their dollars are being spent.

We are going to proceed to questions now and for the most part we will follow in the first round 5 minutes each and then maybe a second time around when we are not as strict on the 5-minute rule.

For Mr. Walker and Ms. Springer, your testimony certainly makes the picture clear. We have made some progress but have a long way to go, and even some of the agencies that have gotten that clean audit, it was through Herculean labor intensive efforts after the fact not internal throughout the year. That is what we really need to get to so any day of the year we can say where are you and we know it as opposed to much afterwards.

I don't expect you to be able to do this today but if you could followup with us and give us your summation of each agency and where they stand in their efforts to modernize and be more accountable. That would help guide this committee where we may need to bring some additional attention from an oversight perspective.

Could you today give us your best opinion on what agency is the closest to having a financial reporting system in place that nears what a large private corporation would have in accounting for their records?

Mr. WALKER. I would note for the record my understanding is the only agency that is green, based upon the President's Management Agenda in financial management is the National Science Foundation. I would imagine that Controller Springer can tell us whether there is anyone else getting close in OMB's view, but I would argue that unless you are green, then you are not even a candidate for being able to give an affirmative to your question.

Ms. SPRINGER. Yes, that is exactly right. The two that are getting close, there are several, the two closest in addition to NSF would be the Social Security Administration and the Environmental Protection Agency that are kind of knocking at the door at that same point.

There are currently 17 of 24 CFO Act agencies that have significant financial management system modernization efforts going on right now. The Government right now invests over 1,900 financial management systems. In the current budget proposal for 2004, there is about $1.5 billion included for financial management systems, so it is a significant effort governmentwide. With the exception of just a few agencies, it is active with all those. Even with that, NSF is the only one today that really meets that standard.

Mr. PLATTS. You are noting 1,900 initiatives or efforts and it seems that speaks to the size of the problem we have, that many initiatives trying to get us on track. Is it also a part of the problem that we have so many diverse efforts as opposed to a more unified, cohesive approach?

Ms. SPRINGER. Yes, it is. I think one of the comments earlier from Representative Towns discussed having solutions that span across a variety of agencies as opposed to just one. One of the strategies we will be looking at will be to find where we can have meaningful joint efforts so that we are not having redundant investments. It seems with financial systems, there ought to be that opportunity, so we will be looking at that.

Mr. PLATTS. Is it going to be your office specifically kind of watching the progress on those 1,900 efforts and birding from OMB's perspective?

Ms. SPRINGER. Yes, along with the IS group headed by Mark Forman. In the CFO Act, the Office of Federal Financial Management has specific responsibility for overseeing those activities and monitoring them as they go forward.

Mr. WALKER. Mr. Chairman, I think it is important to note the Federal Government is a late entrant to the financial management business as well as the financial auditing area. The fact of the matter is that for many, many years, the Federal Government focused all of its time and attention on getting the money and spending the money. It was called the budget. It didn't focus enough on transparency and accountability which is something we need to do now for some of the reasons that I previously articulated.

We have come a long way in a fairly short period of time but we don't have the type of market forces the private sector has. If you are going out there to try to raise stock or if you have publicly traded debt which by the way State and local governments have, so they have had better financial management for years. They have had to have it because in order to be able to have publicly traded debt, in order to get a decent bond rating, they had to have it. We haven't been subject to those same market pressures.

If Brazil can do it, namely have a modern, effective, credible, integrated financial management system for their government, we ought to be able to do it.

Mr. PLATTS. The focus on having that system in place and also renewed focus through PART as the Bush administration asking is not just how much you are spending and where it is coming from but what are we getting in return. That is part of government efficiency as well.

I am going to defer to Mr. Towns now but I would make the analogy in the very frank but stark picture you painted, Mr. Walker, for future years, that I have been one to always balance my checkbook to the penny every month. When my wife and I met, she didn't worry about balancing her checkbook because she knew there was money in there, so she didn't worry month to month. Once we were engaged, married and both graduate students and the excess dollars got less and less, the importance of having a very detailed management system in place, balancing it was more important. That is kind of where we are going as a Federal Government. We look to those out years and we need to make sure every dollar is being used effectively and we know how much we have to spend to set those priorities.

Mr. WALKER. I would respectfully suggest we need to do it now because we are already in deficits.

Mr. PLATTS. Absolutely.

I will now yield to Mr. Towns for the purpose of questions.

Mr. TOWNS. Thank you very much, Mr. Chairman.

Let me thank all of you for your testimony. Let me start with you, Ms. Springer.

You mentioned the fact that the Homeland Security Agency would create a substantial challenge. I was sort of looking at it differently. Maybe you could help me with this, that being it was a new agency, certain things would be put in place that would be able to prevent us from making the mistakes we made in the past. Am I looking at it wrong?

Ms. SPRINGER. No, you are not. I think it is just two aspects. I think starting with a fresh sheet of paper as you described, I think there is that aspect there but at the same time, we are bringing in agencies that have a legacy of history of challenges in their own financial management systems for example and we are not starting from the ground up necessarily with all of those pieces, at least for right now.

In order to meet the financial reporting requirements that we expect of an agency that size and that type of responsibility to the public, we are going to have to use, at least in the interim, some of their own existing systems as at the same time we are building from that clean sheet of paper. I think both aspects are in play right now.

Mr. WALKER. Mr. Towns, I would say it is both a challenge and an opportunity. In the short term, it is a challenge because we have all these non-integrated legacy systems, different cultures, and numerous players that have to be involved, but it is also an opportunity because one would hope we could create enterprise architecture never mind keep the same basis from which you could end up building the future and making all your future IT decisions based upon that so they ought to be able to get to a better place quicker if it is handled the right way.

Short term, it is going to be a big challenge, but it is also an opportunity, as well.

Mr. TOWNS. Thank you. Why is it we have all this problem with DOD?

Mr. WALKER. I would respectfully suggest DOD is an “A” No. 1 in the world in its mission which is fighting and winning armed conflicts; it is a “D” on economy, efficiency, transparency and accountability. It is a “D” for several reasons. One, until recently, it really has not had sustained commitment from the top down. Deputy Secretary Hamry was very interested in this and some of their players. They got started at the end of the last administration but the level of commitment and attention from the top is very evident now, Secretary Rumsfeld down, on this issue. It is being made a priority, with a commitment from the top.

In the past, they have had everybody kind of do their own thing. The Army did its own thing, the Navy, the Air Force, the military side as well as the civilian side. Furthermore, the culture was such that they focused on mission, war fighting. They didn’t focus on basic management and accountability systems and they didn’t have the right type of responsibility and accountability mechanisms in place in order to make sure the people were focusing on them.

One of the things I think Defense needs to do in addition to what they are already doing is they need to think seriously about creating a chief operating officer position or a chief administrative or chief management officer, call it whatever you want, a level two position that focuses day to day on strategic planning and integration of these basic management type functions and activities because they are going to take years and are going to have to span different Secretaries of Defense as well as different Presidents of the United States.

Mr. TOWNS. The privacy issue, how does this play into it? Does this create a problem for you in terms of ascertaining information? Does that issue come up?

Mr. HAMMOND. Let me start as the collector of the government-wide information. I think the information we collect for preparing financial statements either for budget-based reporting or for accrual-based reporting doesn't involve individual privacy concerns. It is done at a high enough level and without identification to individual issues that we have not seen privacy related issues with related financial reporting.

Where we do find it and have to take it very seriously is with regards to the debt collection issues which are another part of the operations of the Financial Management Service, where you are dealing at a more individual level and sometimes dealing with tax-related information. With regard to financial reporting itself, no, we have not experienced any privacy issues.

Ms. SPRINGER. I would say that is also true at the general agency level as well, similar to the debt collection when we initiate some of these improper payment collection activities. That will be another place where we will have to be mindful about privacy issues.

Mr. WALKER. I don't think we have any problems from a financial statement standpoint. I would say one of the things we also have to look at if we are talking about incentives and accountability mechanisms, we need to look at the incentives for people we have overpaid to pay us back in a more timely manner. Right now, the way the law works, if we don't pay promptly, we have to pay interest and penalties but on the other hand, if they get overpaid and don't tell us, they don't suffer any penalty. I would argue that needs to be revisited.

Mr. TOWNS. I see my time has expired, Mr. Chairman.

Mr. PLATTS. Thank you, Mr. Towns.

I will now yield for 5 minutes to our vice chair, Ms. Blackburn from Tennessee.

Ms. BLACKBURN. Thank you, Mr. Chairman. Thank you all for being here today.

I am new to this committee and new to Congress but I am an old hand at State government and led reform initiatives in Tennessee. I look forward to being here and working with you all to be sure that we move toward some efficiency efforts.

Mr. Walker, if my little hen scratching serves me well, as I am sitting here and looking at your chart, which I thank you for, looking at consumption, our composition of spending and where we would be at 2050 and 2030, it looks like at 2030, we would be well over the 50 percent mark for the total expenditure of our citizens on State, local and Federal tax costs. Right now we are pushing the cost of government at about 45 percent when you combine the State, local and Federal cost of government, taxes being the largest budget.

I would recommend and suggest with this in mind that we would soon be crossing that 50 percent threshold that we do have a market force that should be helpful in helping you achieve the goal of reducing the cost of government and that market force would be the taxpayers of the United States who will not stand for over 50 percent of the GDP going to support government.

You each have mentioned material weaknesses in the reporting and accounting measures. My question to each of you is what are you doing to address the material weaknesses in being sure that the reporting and the accounting methods are cleaned up and that we are on the right track? What are your benchmarks, what are your penalties, what is the recommended course of action, and who is responsible for that recommended course of action?

Ms. SPRINGER. Let me take a first answer at that one. The CFO Act agencies in particular which comprise most of the financial statement information, the OMB is meeting with every single agency, every quarter at least and frequently as needed, but very specifically right now coming off this audit, we are asking each agency to give us in writing a plan weakness by weakness for how they are going to deal with it and how they are going to achieve reductions in those weaknesses. We are asking them for plans that have names of individuals who are accountable, we are asking for dates and an actual work plan for having achieved that.

Admittedly, some of those are shorter term fixes that could be remedied within the 1-year horizon. A lot of them will extend a lot longer, particularly the ones related to financial systems.

We also have put up a data base on-line that shows in real time the status of those weaknesses, so it is very transparent, very out in the open. If one of them gets remedied, we go right on-line and fix it but you can drill down from starting from the highest level of here is the total number of weaknesses to the type to a very detailed description and that is maintained. So again, it is very out in the open, there is nothing secretive about it.

Ms. BLACKBURN. What are the penalties if something is not brought into compliance in a given period of time?

Ms. SPRINGER. I think the penalties from this standpoint differ from the private sector I think my colleagues would say as well, that it is not as if you are going out to the marketplace to raise capital and you need to have a clean opinion as if you are dealing with the SEC and you need a clean financial statement.

At the same time, within the administration, I can tell you for a fact, the President will go into the Cabinet meetings and say to Cabinet officers, how come you are still at red. We have a scorecard process of red, yellow and green and one major component is the financial condition inclusive of the material weaknesses and audit opinions for each major Cabinet agency. That is known up to the highest level. There is no greater incentive for a Cabinet Secretary to get their house in order than to know that the President has it on his radar screen.

Ms. BLACKBURN. Mr. Walker.

Mr. WALKER. I think one of the things that has to be considered is the Chief Management Officer/Chief Operating Officer concept at selected departments and agencies and I would respectfully suggest those type of individuals should be term appointments, probably 7 year terms with performance contracts. You would then have accountability for results in this area that span between administrations and I would be happy to talk further about this concept.

The last thing is I agree we have a potential market force, namely the taxpayers. The problem is there are very few people talking about this. A lot of people don't want to talk about this. In fact, if you look at Congress' own budgeting mechanism, you will see decisions are made based upon 1 year and 10 year cash-flow implications, not economic present value, long term implications. As a result, what you get is that a lot of the things Congress is talking about doing will quite frankly make our long term fiscal situation worse not better.

Ms. BLACKBURN. That leads me to another question. As you all can tell, I am one of those geeks who sits around and reads the budget. I really enjoy this stuff and I do want to work with you to be sure the taxpayers are getting a good buy on the government they have. I think that is incredibly important. I think there are far more people that are watching this. I think the Internet has been wonderful to help make government transparent. I applaud you all for trying to move toward a Web-based system, Mr. Hammond as you mentioned.

I did have two questions. Ms. Springer, this may be better to you or to Mr. Hammond, I am not sure.

What do you consider to be the true cost of a piece of legislation when we pass a bill, say like No Child Left Behind, or combining homeland security? As you look at the cost of implementation, do you work through this on a dollar basis or on a percentage basis if this is an $11 billion program, what is that going to cost you to change your accountability standards to put new bureaucracy in place, new management in place? How do you go about estimating that cost of all these good ideas we come up with?

Ms. SPRINGER. I think there are a couple of pieces to that answer. Obviously to the extent there is legislation involved, we would support the scoring process that the Congressional Budget Office has in assigning it a value and a cost figure to any kind of legislative action.

To the extent that we have an investment that doesn't require legislation, an investment in a new system for example, there are case studies required by OMB that will essentially lay out the cost benefit as you would in any other business decision if you are a good business person, private sector trying to bring that same principle to light in the Federal Government so you would go through a very detailed case study to essentially prove the value of that investment.

Ms. BLACKBURN. Right, but I think many times those estimates are quite low going back to what Mr. Walker was saying, that they look at it on a 1 year or 10 year basis and not run it out as you have done.

Ms. SPRINGER. Most of the ones that would come into my realm, if I saw a systems investment, a modernization investment that took 10 years, I would send it back to them and ask them to redo it. Most of mine don't have a very long timeframe.

Mr. HAMMOND. I think if you are looking at entitlement programs or permanent programs, you need to build in an appropriate long-term planning horizon and then do a discounted present value calculation of the net cost based on the assumptions available. That really is what accrual-based reporting supports after the fact but I think the goal would be to try to bring something like that in at the beginning of the process.

Mr. WALKER. I think that is critically important, it is too late after the fact. One example is no matter what you think about the merits of this, the fact is that Congress passed a couple of years ago Tri-care for life for dependents of military personnel. Congress went to the CBO who scored it. They scored it based upon 10 year cash-flow, $50-$60 billion.

We have to deal with discounted present value concepts which is how you ought to make informed decisions. When you look at it on that basis, when we issued the audit report on the financial statements at the end of the year, it wasn't $50-$60 billion in cash-flow, it was $297 billion. The Government would have to have $297 billion today invested in Treasury rates to deliver on that promise.

Congress is thinking about doing the same thing with regard to the issue of not having an offset in connection with VA disability benefits. This is likely to cost even more money and yet Congress doesn't even have the numbers available to it.

For prescription drugs, we are talking about 10 year numbers. Ten year numbers are small change compared to what kind of number we are untimately talking about here. They are just misleading.

Ms. BLACKBURN. Thank you.

Mr. PLATTS. We will come back for an additional round.

I want to followup with Ms. Springer. Mr. Walker talked about a chief management officer and appointment of maybe a fixed term performance contract type position. I would be interested in knowing OMB and the administration's position on such positions specifically for DOD?

Ms. SPRINGER. I think from my perspective, we are interested in getting the right skill sets and the right capabilities applied to the effort. As far as the actual position whether it is a political position or a career position, whether it is a chief operating officer concept, I personally haven't reviewed it but I am sure the administration has a position but my main objective would be to assure that whoever that individual is, they have the right skill set to apply to the problems and get it resolved.

Second, would be the structure, but I am sure there is an administration position on that.

Mr. PLATTS. I agree that having the right people in place who have that drive and whether their political or career is important. If you could followup on what the administration's position would be on the non-political position at DOD that would be great.

Mr. WALKER. If I can provide some information that might be helpful to you and to Linda as well, I have had conversations with Mitch Daniels, with high level DOD officials as well as others on this concept. I know that the Secretary of Defense's Business Process Transformation Advisory Board has recommended the creation of this position. I don't know that the administration has a position yet. I think it would be great for them to have one.

Obviously, they have had some changes in players. Mark Everson, who was involved in the conversation, is now going to be the IRS Commissioner. You have Clay Johnson coming on board. So I look forward to hearing what they have to say.

Mr. PLATTS. It sounds like the Department is embracing it and that goes to the leadership from Secretary Rumsfeld at the top of the department and having that is certainly a good step in the right direction.

Mr. Hammond, Treasury, Social Security and the Postal Service are to be commended for meeting the November 15 deadline 3 months early and really 2 years early. What would be your advice as to the other agencies as to how they could emulate and seek your success in providing that information in a more timely fashion?

Mr. HAMMOND. I think it is an excellent question because what you look at initially is the daunting task of trying to speed up issuing the year-end report. The success story of each of these three agencies indicates it has nothing to do with what you do at the end of the year, but everything to do with what you do during the year.

It really gets to changing the way you look at the data throughout the year, closing your books monthly, analyzing that information to check for trends or inaccuracies and in essence, isolating problems long before the end of the year so that at the end of the year, you are just compiling that which you already understand and know.

You will find in all three of those organizations a strong culture of financial management, a serious commitment beyond just the accounting operations to understanding those numbers and recognizing what they are all about. They come from very different reasons but they share this common theme.

If you look at the Postal Service, they are running a business. They have to know what is going on. Social Security has a huge stewardship responsibility to the American public. They want to have confidence people know their money is being properly managed. The Treasury Department issues the debt on behalf of the Government and collects all the tax revenues, again a huge public responsibility that needs to have credibility. That culture of financial management that kind of seeps throughout all three organizations makes it easier for program agencies to get good information and accept the additional monthly change in business.

Mr. PLATTS. By that internal process, we are not having what Mr. Walker talked about, that end of the year labor intensive catch-up game being needed?

Mr. HAMMOND. Right.

Mr. WALKER. There is still some of that going on at the IRS but they have come a long way and I commend them for their efforts.

I will say one of the other common denominators you have with those three agencies, in addition to what Mr. Hammond said, is committed leadership from the top. For the record, let me note that former Treasury Secretary Paul O'Neill was a person of incredible ability and integrity and was very dedicated to this area. That should be noted.

Ms. SPRINGER. One other comment in this regard. The proof is in the pudding and we have had for the first quarter, for the first time across all 24 agencies, all getting first quarter financial results and financial statements submitted. This was the first year it was required and they all came in on time. Many of those agencies are now going to monthly and also doing full annual statement requirements with footnotes and everything else even though they are not required. It all will support being in a better position at year end.

Mr. PLATTS. I know Mr. Towns is pressed for time and I am going to yield to him. If you need to, take more than 5 minutes to get through your questions.

Mr. TOWNS. On that note, what does that really mean when you say they all got in on time? I am trying to figure out what does that really say? Does that mean they are more committed? What does that really tell you?

Ms. SPRINGER. In order to do just the year-end financial statements, it is possible to work through the course of the year and apply some of these heroic efforts and work over the course of the year's period to be able to get your statements compiled and submitted.

You can't really employ and rely on that kind of effort on a 3-month repeating basis. It really means you have to go back and look at your processes and look at your methodology for developing statement entries because the timeframe is just so much shorter, only 3 months as opposed to 12. The significance of 3 months in getting those in on time is it forces the agency to really break out of that old culture and to adopt new processes. Even if they are still undergoing their systems modernization, there is a lot they can do on the process side. That is what that forces.

Mr. WALKER. One of the primary reasons the JFMIP Principals agreed to accelerate the due date for financial reporting is to take away the option for departments and agencies to engage in these heroic efforts after the end of the year. There is just no way you can engage in these herculean efforts and hit that November 15 date, so that forced them to be able to start dealing with some of the underlying systemic problems. That coupled with having them adopt modern financial management practices, it really isn't rocket science but pretty basic stuff, including quarterly reporting, and you can get a lot of progress pretty quickly.

Mr. TOWNS. Mr. Walker, I think you outlined some of the major problem areas of the Federal Government in achieving a clean opinion. One of these areas, reliability estimating and reporting the liability the government has for environmental remediation and disposal of hazardous waste, this problem is primarily in the Department of Defense. How badly is this area under reported? Are we talking about $1 billion, $10 billion?

Mr. WALKER. Probably tens of billions. It is difficult to say. They have come up with an estimate now but we are not comfortable with their methodology, or the basis of their data. In fact, the DOD now has a process by which each year they have to make a statement to the Inspector General, the Congress and others as to whether or not they believe they are in a position to even have an audit. Last year, they said they were not. This is one of their major challenges, not their only challenge, but it is too early to tell how big the imbalance is. I would say tens of billions.

Mr. TOWNS. I noticed the Department of Energy for a number of years also had problems estimating its environmental liabilities which it has actually corrected. How did they manage to correct their problem and can these solutions be used at the Department of Defense?

Mr. WALKER. I would be happy to provide some additional information for the record. I know they have made progress and would be happy to do that for the record. No doubt one of the things we ought to be doing is looking at where we have had some successes, where we have had progress and what can be done in order to share best practices, along with lessons learned so we can proliferate these throughout government.

Mr. TOWNS. Do you want to add something?

Ms. SPRINGER. I would agree with that and I think we have also employed that best practices sharing in the committee of the CFO Council on Acceleration that Mr. Hammond chairs. We endorse that.

Mr. TOWNS. I want to go back to the whole security privacy question. Are you comfortable with the security system actually being used in terms of the computers being used? Do you feel that is adequately secured in order for you to get the kind of information you really need?

Mr. WALKER. There is a difference between what type of information we need in order to do the audit on the financial statements or to prepare the financial statements which is the executive branch's responsibility. I would note for the record that information security is one of the material control weaknesses governmentwide. It is also an area that is on GAO's high risk list governmentwide as well. So there are issues associated with information security and privacy but they are really not issues that deal with financial reporting and auditing the consolidated financial statements of the U.S. Government.

Mr. TOWNS. I was wondering if through that process inadequate information might come out?

Mr. WALKER. One of the real problems we have in some areas is the lack of timely, accurate and useful information. It is particularly problematic at the Department of Defense because they have thousands of systems by themselves, legacy systems that are nonintegrated. For example, if you look at our high risk series reports, we have one that deals with information security, we have one that deals with DOD financial management, and anouther one that deals with DOD's information technology. It shows an example of how many systems you have to enter one purchase transaction into in order to be able to record it at DOD. I think it is something like 22 times. No wonder we have data problems.

Mr. TOWNS. Are you having difficulty getting information from agencies? Are they cooperating?

Ms. SPRINGER. The level of cooperation is very high. There is no question about that. I would say it is probably at its highest level from what I can tell, but at the same time, they are constrained in providing performance information, if you will, financial performance information by virtue of the cumbersome processes they have in place and systems. So I think there is certainly a willingness to provide information. It is provided but it is the timeliness factor that is not always there. Some of these things took a long time to develop, they are going to take a long time to fix but we are seeing progress. That is what our job is going to be, to make sure that progress continues to completion.

Mr. TOWNS. I guess I am trying to see if there is anything on this side we can do, from the Congress, in terms of any action we might take that might be helpful in terms of being able to obtain the information you need because I see this as being very serious?

Ms. SPRINGER. There is certainly no lack of statutory requirement and existing legislation and requirements for each of the agencies whether it is the Integrity Act and certification of systems, that they are timely and can produce the information and other certifications required by the agency heads around their control environment. I think Congress has certainly done its part in setting forth what the requirements are. The burden is on the agencies to be able to remedy these problems.

Mr. HAMMOND. I think if you look at what the subcommittee is doing today and has done in the past is a great example of where Congress can help, continued oversight and interest in these important issues. It is one thing to have a statutory requirement; it is another thing to have periodic reporting and measurement against the progress to doing that. Certainly agencies are all interested, focused and committed to doing this but I think continued oversight is a very, very helpful way of keeping that focus.

Ms. SPRINGER. If I could add one other thing. Last year, the passage of the Improper Payments Information Act gave, I think, the force of law to the efforts of the executive branch which will improve on that effort significantly. I think that is a good example of a particular area where the legislative support will help us get to the problem a lot sooner.

Mr. TOWNS. I don't want to be guilty of blaming everybody. I think we are all in this together and we have to work together. That is the reason I asked that question.

I yield back, Mr. Chairman. Thank you.

Mr. PLATTS. Thank you, Mr. Towns.

I would note this committee does plan oversight in the near future on SBA and USAID and DOD later this year as well to try to bring some additional oversight to those specific agencies as they work toward their clean audits.

I want to get to the improper payments issue a little, but I want to come back to the DOD issue. Mr. Walker, in your opening statement you talked about being 4½ years into your 15 year term and your hope and expectation that we will have a clean record before your term ends. Clearly, DOD is critical to that achievement. What is your best guesstimate of the process with the leadership we have there now of how soon we could expect DOD to have a financial management system in place that will allow an unqualified audit to begin?

Mr. WALKER. It is going to take several years. The fact of the matter is there is a lot of focus on this, not only within DOD but also within OMB. I participated in more than one meeting on the subject matter within the last several months. DOD is in the process of trying to put together a plan which will be a multiyear plan of what they plan to do in order to address this area.

We are coordinating in a very constructive fashion with the executive branch because obviously they can put together a plan but we are ultimately the ones that have to issue the opinion on the consolidated financial statements of the U.S. Government, so we have to be comfortable with what they are proposing to do as well as the Inspector General of the Department of Defense. I would note for the record the Inspector General was in the last meeting as well. Unless and until that plan is completed and reviewed by all the appropriate parties, it is tough to say but it is going to be several years.

Mr. PLATTS. Does appointment of the Chief Management Officer reduce that in a substantive manner?

Mr. WALKER. It could help but it could help not just in the area of financial management. It could help with regard to providing sustained attention and focus on a range of management issues and to take a more integrated approach to addressing these issues which I think is needed not only within administrations but between administrations. DOD has been in existence for over 56 years and has been on the GAO's high risk list from the very beginning in 1990. It is going to take sustained attention over a period of time to really get to where they need to be.

Ms. SPRINGER. If I could add to that. Having participated in those meetings as well, I have found them to be a good first step. There would be a big leap from no opinion to a clean opinion. The first step, is if we could get this, it would be a fantastic achievement, just to get to a qualified opinion. It is important to recognize there are steps along this process. The DOD system itself is targeted to go live in 2007, so certainly before that it would be a great challenge to be able to make significant progress overall toward getting a qualified opinion. The planning has started now, you don't wait until you get there to plan. You have to look over a period of time.

Mr. WALKER. I think realistically that has to be the plan. You need to try to work toward a qualified opinion before you get to a clean opinion. To note the challenges at DOD, for example, Jeff Steinhoff, our Managing Director for Financial Management and Assurance, just gave me a note saying, "80 percent of the financial information that is needed to do the audit for DOD comes from non-accounting systems." It is all the more important that you take an enterprise-wide, integrated approach to this and you need somebody focused beyond just accounting and financial management. You have to focus on a broader perspective in order to really get the job done. That chief operation officer position would allow that to better happen, bringing all that together.

That is not a slight to the people who are there. Dove Zakheim is truly committed, and Secretary Rumsfeld and Deputy Secretary Wolfowitz are truly committed but they have other things they have to do, too. Realistically, it is going to take a while and we can't keep on changing the players. We must assure that we are making progress and have appropriate accountability for results.

Mr. PLATTS. Taking the DOD experience to DHS, and some of the previous questions touched on not getting behind the eight ball with DHS, while acknowledging that we are bringing together a lot of existing agencies that have problems. DHS is not covered under the CFO Act. Would it be your recommendation that they should be statutorily required to further comply with that act?

Ms. SPRINGER. DHS, as other agencies not covered by the CFO Act, are subject to the Accountability of Taxpayers Act enacted last year. So they do have a requirement to produce audited annual financial statements. In that respect, they are not exempt. I think whether it is that act or whether the CFO Act, for an agency of that size there is a very high bar and standard they need to meet. So we have talked with them about producing the quarterly financial statements that are required of the CFO Act agencies every bit as much as if they were. They do have a reporting requirement.

Mr. PLATTS. Having that quarterly requirement I think goes to Mr. Towns' comment that we up front start on the right foot instead of trying to play catchup.

Mr. Towns, did you have other questions?

Mr. TOWNS. No.

Mr. PLATTS. I am going to turn to the Improper Payments Act and implementation of that. We heard $20 billion, $35 billion. Is there any additional insight on the amount? As a guy who lives in a community where you can still get a 99 cents breakfast special, $35 billion every year of improper payments is staggering to me.

Mr. TOWNS. Where is that?

Mr. PLATTS. Come on up, Mr. Towns. My guess is if that is what we are thinking, it is probably more. Would you hazard to guess how much higher we may find it to be?

Ms. SPRINGER. I will give you some figures that helped me put it into perspective and I think would lead you to the answer. The $35 billion was based on a base of payments of about $900 billion, so the rate is roughly 3.9 percent, close to 4 percent. There is a budget of $2 trillion, so there is another $1.1 trillion that hasn't even been measured yet. Admittedly that is not all going to be erroneous but if you apply that same type of percentage, there is a lot more money yet there that is likely to raise that $35 billion.

Mr. PLATTS. Maybe another $15-$20 billion if you applied the percentage?

Ms. SPRINGER. I think that is conservative. I think we are going to see that number go higher but you have to diagnose the illness, not before but as you are curing it, you need to know the extent of the illness. We find that number is going up and I think it will go up.

Mr. PLATTS. With your efforts in addressing that, I know with every agency having to identify what their improper payments are, OMB is working, and in your testimony you talked about proposed common sense approaches for student financial assistance. How far along is OMB with each agency in trying to get them in good shape for making that more definitive identification occur?

Ms. SPRINGER. Two things. For the budget, the 2004 budget is part of that process. We asked agencies kind of in advance or in anticipation of the act for identifying their baseline of erroneous payments and what efforts are being made. The response was mixed. I would say about half the agencies had things in the works. So there is a long way to go there.

OMB is also on target to issue its guidance related to the act. That is due by the end of May. We will get that out and that will require some very specific action steps related to estimating and showing progress.

Mr. PLATTS. The end of May?

Ms. SPRINGER. The end of May is the due date.

Mr. WALKER. I think there is no question it is higher than $35 billion. I think the act passed by the Congress last year will only help us to ascertain what the number is but I think it is important to note that progress is being made. For example, at the Center for Medicare/Medicaid Services, when the first improper payment estimate was done, that agency was over $20 billion. I think last year it was down about $12–$13 billion, still unacceptable and still too high but they have made a considerable amount of progress in that regard. So we need to know what the base is to have focused attention on it.

I think it is also important to note what improper payments are and what they aren't. Some of these are duplicate payments you need to recover; some of these are payments where we don't know whether they were proper or not because we don't have the adequate documentation. So it is not all fraud, waste and abuse. It is not money that is down the drain. Some of it is, but we need to focus more attention on this area in order to solve the problem.

Mr. PLATTS. Ms. Springer, you identified with the earned income tax credit that the proposal to spend $100 million to try to better explain the tax credit so we can save the $9 billion that we think we are overpaying and if those efforts are successful, those are going to be great.

When you talk about the proposals with eligibility for applicants for student financial aid, you say you proposed those. How have they been received?

Ms. SPRINGER. Some of those are still in the works. For example, where there is an opportunity to have access to a tax data base or where there is an opportunity to have access to a new hires data base. So some of those just in the past month have come up to the Hill for discussion.

Mr. PLATTS. So you are still kind of in the early stage?

Ms. SPRINGER. Early stage, yes. They have been met with good receptivity.

Mr. PLATTS. This is a question for all three but it starts with Treasury. In your 2001 and 2002 consolidated financial statements, there was roughly $17 billion each year that was unreconciled transactions and that is how the $17.1 billion and $17.3 billion amounts in each year were identified to really reconcile the Treasury books. What does that mean? Is that money that was lost, we just don't know what happened to it, is it part of improper payments? What is your best estimate of what that accounts for?

Mr. HAMMOND. We think that it is the various balances that are misidentified between the agencies dealing with business taking place between themselves. When you are pulling together a consolidated financial statement across various organizations, you have to make sure you eliminate the activity that takes place internally because otherwise, you will be overstating to the public the net results of the joint activity. As we go about that, it is inherent on proper data quality and data identification coming into the system.

To give you an example, this year we put together a system to be able to compare based on trading partner information, the various components of activity between the various parts of agencies. When we went back and forth and looked at what agency A said they did in business with agency B and what agency B acknowledged they did in business with agency A, when we compared all that, we had a net difference of $55 billion. That gives you a rough order of magnitude of the idea that the data coming in isn't properly classified and in many cases, frankly, isn't booked the same way on both sides of the transaction.

Mr. PLATTS. Does that go to the internal control issue, if they are $55 billion off?

Mr. HAMMOND. There is an internal control aspect to it, there is also a data identification aspect to it. Some agencies look at other agencies as being the same thing as the public, so it is hard for them to pull out of their systems and differentiate between activity they do outside the government and activity they do inside the government.

The third piece of it is they treat data differently. For example, some agencies will book a receivable for business they are doing with other agencies but the other agency may not book a payable.

Mr. PLATTS. It is comparing apples and oranges, how the different agencies look at the same information. There is not a unified analysis of how they credit it which accounts for different treatment in their books.

Mr. HAMMOND. Exactly, so we have done a couple of things over the years to narrow that problem as well as to try to isolate the differences and then deal with those. We have with regard to the large dollar components, the investment activity that agencies have buying Treasury securities, the funding for the Civil Service Pension Program, isolated those and resolved or explained virtually all of those differences. We are now left to the routine activity between the agencies and to do that, OMB issued some intergovernmental business rules this summer that have gone into effect to create standardized business practices all agencies will have to follow. The second piece is that there is a joint agency effort building a system for the commercial activities between agencies that will hopefully capture and record all that information at the point of initiation and go a long way to solving that. It is a fairly daunting task.

Mr. PLATTS. Hopefully as we get to more transparency and credible testimony or evidence because to the person looking at that, you balance, but there is this $17 billion sum that is unreconciled. The more we can reconcile; the more credible the balance statements will be.

Mr. WALKER. In accounting parlance, it is referred to as a plug but it is a $17.1 billion plug, which is a net number. We don't know what the gross number is. It is the net number, the net difference. It is something that has to be resolved. I do agree with Mr. Hammond it is primarily dealing with these intragovernmental transactions we need to get our arms around and that is too high.

Mr. PLATTS. Ms. Springer talked about the formal process of having across the board treatment of those intergovernmental transfers.

Ms. SPRINGER. Right and that was a large part, and I can't take any credit for it, but getting out these rules and getting the system support for catching all those things.

Mr. HAMMOND. It may be a small sense of comfort, and I prefer the term my Canadian colleagues use for their plug in their financial statements which is a harmonizing entry. [Laughter.]

Mr. WALKER. It is a plug. You can't make it sound like it is not.

Mr. HAMMOND. You will notice it is actually an addition, not a cost, actually a negative cost in the statements, again providing some sense that it is intragovernmental activity, if properly eliminated, would hopefully explain that.

Mr. PLATTS. I apologize; I am listening. I am supposed to be in a mark-up and they are telling me that I am voting but now they tell me the vote is over, so I don't have to run off, the usual of being in two or three places at once.

Harmonizing plug?

Mr. HAMMOND. It is the same thing.

Mr. PLATTS. And we all share the hope that we stop plugging but just reporting and certainly steps like the uniform approach to these transfers is a step in the right direction so we are all on the same page.

Mr. Hammond, with that part sounding more specifically related to the transfers, when we talk about improper payment specifically with Treasury as far as your history, are there any obstacles Treasury sees to having more success in avoiding improper payments?

Mr. HAMMOND. The biggest improper payment I am familiar with at the Treasury Department deals with the earned income tax credit at the IRS. I think that is a very daunting task because part of the reason there is a level of improper payments with regard to that category has to do with the design of the program itself. It is driven the way it is statutorily created and the way it has to be administered in the Tax Code puts certain barriers on the effective management of the actual improper payment amount.

One of the questions you have to look at as we dig deeper into improper payments and look at them with regard to various programs is the cost benefit analysis related to reaching a point of zero or minimal improper payments. If you look at any business today, you will find they have certain losses. There is an unacceptable level of loss and an acceptable level of loss. They make that judgment based on the cost related to get below that threshold.

The Government is not to that point I don't think in being able to assess the various programs on improper payments but at some point we will have to get there and understand at what point do you say, it will cost so much more to go from this level to this level that we have to live with that or alternatively, redesign the program. I think the EITC is kind of a case study in that.

Mr. PLATTS. With the hope to spend the $100 million to address that, are we going to be closely scrutinizing the cost benefit of that $100 million, is it actually going to reduce that $9 billion in improper payments? I assume that would be part of that process?

Ms. SPRINGER. That is right. Actually before that even got into the budget, I had the opportunity to sit in and kind of audit that session. Clearly the expectation on the investment of $100 million, while it is not a small number, is to make a significant dent in what right now is a $9 billion problem.

Mr. PLATTS. For all three of you on the Medicare fee for service, $12 billion, 6.3 percent of improper payments identified, while we want to aggressively go after any improper payments, Mr. Walker you kind of identified this, some of that may not be improper. We just don't know.

I spend every couple of months, and it is harder to do now than when I was in the State House, but a day on the job with a constituent. I have had great experiences with truck drivers, postal workers, teachers, you name it. One day I spent in an emergency room with a physician and staff nurses for a 12-hour shift. Part of that day was watching the emergency department physician do recordkeeping for Medicare. The concern he expressed about improper payments is that while we are trying to identify them that we do so in a responsible way. His point was he was sitting here today identifying what he believes is a proper treatment and that translates to where they fall as far as reimbursement. Nine months from now Medicare would come back and say you were intentionally defrauding the government and it should have been level 3 not level 4 and the burden is on the physician to prove they were right.

Do you see anything that raises concerns as we go after improper payments that we need to keep our eye on that we are not doing in a wrongful way and being overzealous and maybe trying to recoup money not improper but not appropriately identified?

Ms. SPRINGER. That situation is certainly not the intent of any of these programs. It is just to go after whether it is fraud, waste or abuse, or inefficiencies or just getting better information to know where we stand. It certainly wouldn't be to comprise the integrity of any of the programs or the intent of the mission of the programs.

Mr. WALKER. The other thing you have to look at is that obviously the act passed last year was intended to increase the amount of transparency, the amount of light associated with these amounts. You manage what you measure, so until you start measuring it, you are not going to be able to effectively manage it.

The other thing we have to do is look at what types of incentives and accountability mechanisms can be put in place if it turns out that there were behaviors or actions that were inappropriate. I come back to what I said before. If we made a duplicate payment, after a certain period of time I would expect that if somebody economically benefited from that, we ought to be able to recover some of that benefit. Maybe for some major contractors, we ought to require them to tell us after a period of time.

Also to the extent it turns out there is improper upcoding, what that refers to, if it is innocent it is one thing but if there is intentional upcoding, I think you have to more sanction than just getting the money back. That is not enough to prevent undesirable behavior.

There has to be reasonable transparency, appropriate incentives for people to do the right thing and assured accountability when they don't do the right thing. If you don't have that, the system is not going to work.

Mr. PLATTS. There has to be a consequence.

I am going to wrap up with a final question. Mr. Walker, talking about us getting to maybe 10 years that clean, consolidated financial report, I would be interested with OMB and Treasury if you want to guesstimate from your perspectives and in a broad sense what is the biggest hurdle or obstacle that it is going to take 10 years? Is it just because DOD is such a big part of getting our arms around that it is going to take so long?

Mr. WALKER. First, since we are the ones who have to express the opinion, I would say I hope and expect that no later than the end of my term we will be in a position to issue a clean opinion, but that is going to require sustained commitment and attention not only within the executive branch but also in the Congress in order to make that happen. We have made a lot of progress over the last several years. At the same point in time, that progress could quickly wane if the executive branch or Congress do not continue to be dually committed to this effort. People could easily go back to where they were before.

It could be quicker than that. I think realistically we are going to see a qualified opinion before we get to a clean opinion and it is too early to tell when it is going to be.

Ms. SPRINGER. One week into this position, I am certainly not going to go out on a limb with a date but I would say it will take a consistent sustained effort by certainly the executive branch. Plans are in place. Clearly the first objective is going to be a qualified opinion. To the extent we can lay the groundwork for a qualified opinion, then we go to a clean opinion. The challenge is there. DOD understands. We understand what our material weaknesses are.

We would like to think within a couple of years we could be talking or planning for working with GAO toward getting that qualified opinion, within a shorter timeframe than 10 years. Qualified is within our sight. However, that is not to say it isn't a major task. It is a cultural issue. You can have the best systems in the world, the best processes in the world, but unless you have a culture that is the best of the private sector approach for this thing, you couldn't achieve it. I think it is doable. I think a qualified opinion is certainly within the next couple of years or so. I think we could be planning toward that.

Mr. HAMMOND. As my colleagues will tell you, I have been known for my unbridled optimism, so I will continue to be optimistic.

It is my sense that as we are working to resolve the governmentwide issues dealing with preparation of the report and the intergovernmental transactions and data quality, DOD will continue to make progress in specific areas. The combination of those two items should position us within the next few years to get a qualified opinion. The state of those remaining DOD issues will then determine how qualified that opinion may be, but I think that it is certainly not going to be 2003 but I do believe we can see a qualified opinion in a realistic time period.

Mr. PLATTS. I share the optimistic approach day in and day out and hope we are right. I will tell you as the new Chair of this committee, I am encouraged by things like the Improper Payments Act that everybody now is going to put a number for their agency, what is it so we can, as you say, manage once we think we know what the number is.

The President's Management Agenda in total, the PART program evaluation are all positive signs that encourage me to be optimistic that we are heading in the right direction. As a committee, we certainly look forward to working with each of you and the administration to have more transparency and more accountability. As we started the meeting with Mr. Walker's testimony, it is a necessity for what is coming down the pike in the years to come when my children and future generations are going to be challenged financially to deal with the needs of our citizens.

In closing, I want to thank our great staff on both the majority and minority side for their work in putting together this hearing. Again, let me thank each of you for your written testimony, your comments here today and the followup materials you will be sharing with us.

Based on the testimony we have heard today and also at the previous two hearings, it is evident that agencies are increasingly placing more emphasis on financial management. Today we are especially pleased with the Treasury Department's example of accelerating the issuance of its audited financial statements to November, 2 years ahead of the required timeframe. It is my hope that other agencies are going to follow and we don't have to wait for 2 more years. One year out maybe we will have a few more not just the three that were ahead of the game this time. We are moving in the right direction but we all remain concerned about the financial management practices of agencies that did not receive unqualified opinions. As I mentioned earlier, later this month we will be having a hearing with the Small Business Administration and in early May, with USAID to try to bring some more light, some more attention and get to the bottom of what their challenges are. It is my hope these agencies will give us some insight from within of how they are working to rectify their inability to receive unqualified opinions.

We will hold the record open for 2 weeks from this date for those who want to forward submissions for inclusion.

This meeting stands adjourned.

[Whereupon, at 12:23 p.m., the subcommittee was adjourned, to reconvene at the call of the Chair.]

[Additional information submitted for the hearing record follows:]

GAO
Accountability * Integrity * Reliability

Comptroller General
of the United States

United States General Accounting Office
Washington, DC 20548

June 16, 2003

The Honorable Todd R. Platts
Chairman
Subcommittee on Government Efficiency
and Financial Management
Committee on Government Reform
House of Representatives

Subject: *Responses to Posthearing Questions Related to GAO's Testimony on the U.S. Government's Consolidated Financial Statements for Fiscal Year 2002*

Dear Mr. Chairman:

On April 8, 2003, I testified before your subcommittee at a hearing on our report on the U.S. government's consolidated financial statements for fiscal year 2002.[1] This letter responds to questions related to our testimony from you and the Ranking Minority Member and to subsequent questions from the Vice Chairman that you asked us to answer for the record. The questions and my responses follow.

Question from Chairman Platts

1. What is the status of the financial management systems modernization effort, agency by agency?

At a meeting with subcommittee counsel and staff on April 16, we agreed on an approach based primarily on available data sources and an end-of-June time frame for separately providing this information. We will compile a list of the 24 Chief Financial Officers (CFO) Act agencies' core financial systems along with key data related to each system, such as whether it is a commercial off-the-shelf system. We will identify the status of agencies' plans to acquire new core financial systems and whether any mixed financial systems at the agencies are slated to be updated.

[1] U.S. General Accounting Office, *Fiscal Year 2002 U.S. Government Financial Statements: Sustained Leadership and Oversight Needed for Effective Implementation of Financial Management Reform,* GAO-03-572T (Washington, D.C.: Apr. 8, 2003). The fiscal year 2002 *Financial Report of the United States Government,* issued by the Department of the Treasury on March 31, 2003, is available through GAO's Web site at www.gao.gov and Treasury's Web site at www.fms.treas.gov/fr/index.html.

Question from Ranking Minority Member Towns

1. The Department of Energy for a number of years had problems estimating its environmental liabilities, which it has since corrected. How did Energy manage to correct its problem, and can these solutions be used at the Department of Defense?

The Department of Energy (DOE) is responsible for management and cleanup of environmental contamination related to the process of producing nuclear weapons. For fiscal year 1998, the DOE Inspector General's (IG) financial audit opinion stated that auditors were unable to satisfy themselves that DOE's recorded environmental liability of $186 billion was fairly stated because of the following deficiencies:

- DOE lacked adequate documentation to support some cost estimates and cost-estimating methodologies.
- Valid environmental liabilities were not included in the estimate.
- Cost estimates had not been updated through the end of the fiscal year under audit.
- Established cost-estimating guidelines were not consistently applied.

For fiscal year 1999, the DOE IG was able to conclude that DOE's reported $231 billion environmental liability was fairly stated. According to the DOE IG, DOE's Office of Environmental Management completed corrective actions during fiscal year 1999 that included strengthening internal controls over developing the estimate; assessing individual cost estimates that make up the environmental liability in terms of scope, cost, and schedule; and quantifying the uncertainty of the estimates caused by technical problems and funding shortfalls. To ensure the reliability of future environmental liability estimates and to guide cleanup efforts, DOE developed a program, which it documented in the June 1998 publication *Accelerated Cleanup: Paths to Closure,* based on site-developed, project-by-project forecasts of the scope, schedule, and costs to complete DOE's approximately 350 projects. The objective was to manage the cleanup of 90 percent of contaminated sites by 2006. This program, which had the support of top management, was key to DOE's success.

The Department of Defense (DOD) is responsible for management and cleanup of very diverse types of environmental contamination, including

- closed and open sites where past and current waste disposal practices, leaks, spills, and other activities have created a risk to public health or the environment;
- closed, transferring, and active military ranges where contamination and unexploded ordnance create environmental hazards; and
- cleanup, demilitarization, and disposal of nuclear and non-nuclear weapons systems, chemical weapons, and munitions.

Although the types of cleanup are different, the obstacles to reliable cost estimation are similar to those faced by DOE in fiscal year 1998. For the past few years, the DOD IG has reported that the environmental liability figure reported in DOD's financial statements is not auditable because of problems related to insufficient guidance, lack of audit trails, use of inconsistent or unvalidated cost-estimating models, and incomplete inventories of sites. We have also cited deficiencies in DOD's reported environmental liabilities as a disclaimer issue in the governmentwide audit reports since fiscal year 1997, and we have issued reports on several kinds of environmental cleanup issues, including training ranges and ongoing operations.[2]

In its fiscal year 2002 performance and accountability report, DOD management included a discussion of progress being made to address material weaknesses, including environmental liabilities. According to the report, DOD

- has issued improved guidance—for all areas except ongoing operations—that will help its components compile complete, accurate, and fully substantiated environmental liability data;
- is developing and maintaining adequate supporting documentation and audit trails for cost-to-complete estimates for the environmental restoration of more than 30,000 closed contaminated sites on open installations, closed installations, and Base Realignment and Closure sites;
- has validated the cost-estimating models used in the calculation and documentation of environmental liability costs;
- has developed a sound methodology for estimating liabilities associated with nuclear-powered ships and submarines; and
- has completed inventories of all but training ranges and sites with ongoing operations that result in contamination.

DOD has also reviewed *Paths to Closure* and believes that DOE's approach is similar to that used by DOD to estimate and report for the Defense Environmental Restoration Program (DERP). DOD reports site-by-site information in its DERP report to Congress each year and estimates cleanup costs for those sites out to the year 2030. DOD has stated that it has also begun reconciling the DERP reported costs to the financial statement reported costs. Finally, DOD has designated the Deputy Under Secretary of Defense (Installations and Environment) as the focal point for all environmental restoration and cleanup issues except for chemical demilitarization, which is the responsibility of the Under Secretary of Defense (Acquisition, Technology and Logistics).

DOD claims that various components of its environmental cleanup and disposal costs are now auditable. For fiscal year 2003, the DOD IG plans to review the Navy's methodology for estimating liabilities associated with nuclear-powered ships and submarines and also to audit the Army's chemical demilitarization cost estimates.

---

[2]U.S. General Accounting Office, *Environmental Liabilities: DOD Training Range Cost Estimates Are Likely Understated,* GAO-01-479 (Washington, D.C.: Apr. 11, 2001), and *Environmental Liabilities: Cleanup Costs from Certain DOD Operations Are Not Being Reported,* GAO-02-117 (Washington, D.C.: Dec. 14, 2001).

Questions from Vice Chairman Blackburn Submitted on April 24

1. What are your recommendations to arrest spending on Medicare/Medicaid and Social Security?

As I have testified on numerous occasions before various committees, reducing the relative future burdens of Social Security and health programs is critical to promoting a sustainable budget policy for the longer term.[3] While much of the public debate concerning the Social Security and Medicare programs focuses on trust fund balances—that is, on the programs' solvency—the larger issue concerns program sustainability. Absent reform, the impact of federal health and retirement programs on budget choices will be felt long before projected trust fund insolvency dates when the cash needs of these programs begin to seriously constrain overall budgetary flexibility.

Early action to change these programs would yield the highest fiscal dividends for the federal budget and would provide a longer period for prospective beneficiaries to make adjustments in their own planning. Waiting to build economic resources and reform future claims entails risks. First, we lose an important window where today's relatively large workforce can increase saving and enhance productivity, two elements critical to growing the future economy. Second, we lose the opportunity to reduce the burden of interest payments, thereby creating a legacy of higher debt as well as elderly entitlement spending for the relatively smaller workforce of the future. Finally, and most critically, we risk losing the opportunity to phase in changes gradually so that all can make the adjustments needed in private and public plans to accommodate this historic shift.

Unfortunately, the long-range challenge has become more difficult, and the window of opportunity to address the entitlement challenge is narrowing. In fact, the leading edge of the baby boom generation will become eligible for Social Security in only 5 years. As baby boomers retire and the numbers of those entitled to these retirement benefits grow, the difficulties of reform will be compounded. Accordingly, it remains more important than ever to deal with these issues over the next several years.

Many proposals to control spending, increase revenues, and restructure Social Security and Medicare have been put forth by various commissions, members of Congress, and independent "think tanks." Although we do not make specific policy recommendations, to assist Congress in its deliberations, we have developed criteria for evaluating Social Security reform proposals and soon will issue criteria for evaluating health care reforms. Our criteria for evaluating Social Security reform proposals aim to balance financial and economic considerations with benefit adequacy and equity issues and the administrative challenges associated with various

[3]See, for example, U.S. General Accounting Office, *Medicare: Financial Challenges and Considerations for Reform,* GAO-03-577T (Washington, D.C.: Apr. 10, 2003); *Medicare: Observations on Program Sustainability and Strategies to Control Spending on Any Proposed Drug Benefit,* GAO-03-650T (Washington, D.C.: April 9, 2003); *Social Security: Analysis of Issues and Selected Reform Proposals,* GAO-03-376T (Washington, D.C.: Jan. 15, 2003); *Budget Issues: Long-Term Fiscal Challenges,* GAO-02-467T (Washington, D.C.: Feb. 27, 2002).

proposals. The use of these criteria can help facilitate fair consideration and informed debate of reform proposals. The weight that different policymakers may place on different criteria will vary, depending on how they value different attributes.

The proposals we have examined, both in 2002 and earlier, reflect the likelihood that the structural changes required to restore Social Security's long-term viability generally may require some combination of reductions from currently scheduled benefits and revenue increases, and may include the use of some general revenues.[4] Proposals employ possible benefit reductions within the current program structure, including modifying the benefit formula, raising the retirement age, and reducing cost-of-living adjustments. Revenue increases might take the form of increases in the payroll tax rate and/or wage base, expanding coverage to include the relatively few workers who are still not covered under Social Security, or allowing the trust funds to be invested in potentially higher-yielding securities, such as stocks. Similarly, some proposals rely on general revenue transfers to increase the amount of money going toward the Social Security program. Some proposals include individual accounts that would also involve Social Security benefit reductions and/or revenue increases.

Medicare also faces a long-range, fundamental, and more serious financing problem driven by known demographic trends and projected escalation of health care spending beyond general inflation. As with Social Security, Medicare reform would be done best with considerable lead time to phase in changes and before the changes that are needed become dramatic and disruptive. Given the size of Medicare's financial challenge, it is only realistic to expect that reforms intended to bring down future costs will have to proceed incrementally. We should begin this now, when retirees are still a far smaller proportion of the population than they will be in the future. The sooner we get started, the less difficult the task will be.

We should also remember that the sources of some of Medicare's problems—and its solutions—are outside the program and are universal to all health care payers. Some tax preferences mask the full cost of providing health benefits and can work at cross-purposes to the goal of moderating health care spending. Therefore, it may be important to reexamine the incentives contained in current tax policy and consider potential reforms. Advances in medical technology are also likely to keep raising the price tag of providing care, regardless of the payer. Although technological advances unquestionably provide medical benefits, judging the value of those benefits—and weighing them against the additional costs—is more difficult. Consumers are not as informed about the cost of health care and its quality as they may be about other goods and services. Thus, while the greater use of market forces may help to control cost growth, it will undoubtedly be necessary to employ additional transparency and cost control methods as well. Ultimately, we will need to look at broader health care reforms to balance health care spending with other societal priorities. In doing this, it is important to note the fundamental differences between health care wants, which

[4]See, for example, U.S. General Accounting Office, *Social Security Reform: Analysis of Reform Models Developed by the President's Commission to Strengthen Social Security*, GAO-03-310 (Washington, D.C.: Jan. 15, 2003), and *Social Security: Evaluating Reform Proposals*, GAO/AIMD/HEHS-00-29 (Washington, D.C., Nov. 4, 1999).

are virtually unlimited; needs, which should be defined and addressed; and overall affordability and sustainability, of which there is a limit.

We are preparing a health care framework that includes a set of principles to help policy makers in their efforts to assess various health financing reform options. This framework will examine health care issues systemwide and identify the interconnections between public programs that finance health care and the private insurance market. The framework can serve as a tool for defining policy goals and ensuring the use of consistent criteria for evaluating changes. By facilitating debate, the framework can encourage acceptance of changes necessary to put us on a path to fiscal sustainability.

For Medicare and Medicaid, the sustainability challenge has three levels—the level of the individual programs, the health care system in which they are embedded, and our long-term federal fiscal challenge. GAO's long-term budget simulations continue to show that to move into the future with no changes to federal health and retirement programs is to envision a very different role for the federal government. Assuming, for example, that the tax reductions enacted in 2001 do not sunset and discretionary spending keeps pace with the economy, by midcentury federal revenues may not even be adequate to pay Social Security and interest on the federal debt. To obtain budget balance, massive spending cuts, tax increases, or some combination of the two would be necessary. Neither slowing the growth of discretionary spending nor allowing the tax reductions to sunset eliminates the imbalance. In addition, while economic growth would help ease our burden, the projected fiscal gap is too great for us to grow our way out of the problem.

2. What is your recommended course of action to address the true cost of new legislation (for example, veterans' benefits, prescription drug plans)?

Current budget reporting is not always designed to promote the recognition and explicit consideration of the costs of some policies and programs. For example, the government undertakes a wide range of responsibilities, policies, programs, and activities that may obligate it to future spending or simply create an expectation for such spending. These "fiscal exposures" range from explicit liabilities to implicit promises embedded in current policy or public expectations. The examples you cite of new legislation for veterans' benefits or prescription drug plans could be viewed as creating new fiscal exposures. We have made the following recommendations[5] to increase the visibility and transparency of such exposures:

- First, we recommend that OMB report the future estimated costs associated with certain exposures as a new budget concept—"exposure level"—as a notational item in the Program and Financing schedule of the President's budget. As opposed to cash, the "exposure level" might be reported in present value terms.

[5]U.S. General Accounting Office, *Fiscal Exposures: Improving the Budgetary Focus on Long-Term Costs and Uncertainties,* GAO-03-213 (Washington, D.C.: Jan. 24, 2003).

Specifying the estimated potential future costs associated with current decisions would promote transparency.

- We also recommend that OMB report annually on fiscal exposures, including a concise list and description of such exposures, cost estimates where possible, and an assessment of methodologies and data used to produce the cost estimates. Explicitly and directly integrating this report with long-range projections and analysis of the budget as a whole would increase its usefulness for assessing the potential implications for long-range fiscal sustainability and flexibility. Legislation proposed by the President could be included if the report were issued as part of the President's budget and thus could help inform and provide long-term context to budget deliberations.

Other entities also can promote transparency and visibility of fiscal exposures by various actions:

- FASAB. Continue to make progress on the accounting and reporting front (e.g., trust funds and social insurance).
- Treasury. Enhance disclosures in the annual governmentwide performance and accountability report.
- GAO. Continue to emphasize the issue in existing reports and testimonies. Comment on any annual fiscal exposures report published by OMB.
- Congress. Consider requiring that discounted present value numbers be considered for major revenue- and spending-related legislative proposals before legislation is enacted.

In addition, we have stated that Congress may wish to consider exploring options for improving the information available on and the attention given to fiscal exposures.[6] To increase congressional attention to such exposures, Congress could develop budget process mechanisms that prompt more deliberation about fiscal exposures. One type of mechanism that could be used is a point of order. Congress could modify budget rules to provide for a point of order against any proposed legislation that creates new exposures or increases the estimated costs of existing exposures over some specified level. Or, revised rules could provide for a point of order against any proposed legislation that does not include estimates of the potential costs of fiscal exposures created by the legislation. A second type of budget process mechanism that would prompt deliberation of fiscal exposures would be to establish triggers that require some action when the estimated future costs of a given exposure rise above some specified threshold.

3. How are audit results being used to affect budgeting processes for the current and next year, and how should they be used?

Ultimately, the objective is for agencies to generate high-quality data and measure performance in a meaningful way to help inform decision makers during the budget

[6]GAO-03-213.

process when allocating resources and determining the most efficient and effective means of achieving policy objectives. Financial audit results are the beginning point in this process and should be considered along with the results of programmatic audits and performance reviews.

Financial statements are included in the annual performance and accountability reports for the 24 CFO Act agencies. These financial statements, along with the accompanying management analysis and performance reports, can provide a wealth of information regarding agency performance and financial condition that can be considered as budgeting decisions are made. One of the objectives of federal financial management reform legislation is to improve the quality and availability of information for decision makers. The results of agency financial statement audits, including the related identification of any internal control weaknesses, noncompliance, and systems issues, provide the starting point for considering an agency's ability to generate the information necessary to make informed decisions about its efficiency and effectiveness in achieving its mission and goals. For fiscal year 2002, while 21 of the 24 CFO Act agencies received an unqualified opinion on their financial statements, auditors for 19 of the 24 agencies reported that the agencies' systems did not comply substantially with at least one of the three requirements of the Federal Financial Management Improvement Act. This lack of compliance raises questions about the ability of these agencies to generate timely, useful, and reliable information needed for day-to-day management and congressional oversight.

The audited financial statements also provide indications of the quality of certain data included in budget requests and historical information that could be considered during budget deliberations. For example, the Statement of Budgetary Resources in the agency's audited financial statements provides information as to the status and uses of budgetary resources, such as amounts remaining available for obligation as of the end of the fiscal year. Because this information is audited, it provides assurance as to the reliability of these amounts in relation to the financial statements as a whole. In areas such as direct loans and loan guarantees, the accounting used for the financial statements under generally accepted accounting principles closely mirrors the Credit Reform Act requirements used for the budget. This means that errors, weaknesses in the estimation process, or other issues identified during the financial statement audit may also be present in related budget requests.

In addition, the audited financial statements provide information not presented in the budget that could also be considered in the budgeting process. For example, liabilities for the total estimated cost of environmental cleanup and other liabilities, such as those for federal employees' and veterans' benefits, are presented in the financial statements. These amounts should include the entire estimated liability for these programs, rather than the projected cash flows for limited periods included in the budget. Further, the statements present information on social insurance programs, such as Social Security and Medicare, that shows the long-term fiscal challenges associated with these programs that could also be considered in the budget process. While much of this information is included in individual agency financial statements, the presentation of this information in the consolidated financial report of the U.S. government can provide a basis for analyzing the overall long-range fiscal challenges faced by our government as a whole, during the deliberative process on the budget.

The audited financial statements present data as of a single point in time or for a specific period. Even if an agency's financial statements received an unqualified opinion, there are no direct assurances about other data from the agency, such as quarterly results or performance information. However, as part of the audits, material weaknesses in internal control and inadequate financial systems are often identified. These deficiencies can affect an agency's ability to generate reliable cost information and measure the performance of its programs. The impact of these conditions on the reliability of other, unaudited agency data should be considered from an oversight or budget perspective.

I am providing copies of this letter to the Ranking Minority Member and Vice Chairman of your subcommittee. This letter is also available on GAO's Web site at www.gao.gov.

If you or your staff have questions about the responses to your questions, please contact me at (202) 512-5500 or Gary T. Engel, Director, at (202) 512-3406 or engelg@gao.gov.

Sincerely yours,

David M. Walker
Comptroller General
of the United States

(198195)

MAY-16-03 16:23 FROM:OMB ID: PAGE 2/4

EXECUTIVE OFFICE OF THE PRESIDENT
OFFICE OF MANAGEMENT AND BUDGET
WASHINGTON, D.C. 20503

OFFICE OF FEDERAL
FINANCIAL MANAGEMENT

May 16, 2003

The Honorable Todd Russell Platts
1032 Longworth House Office Building
Washington, DC 20515

Dear Congressman Platts:

Enclosed, please find answers to questions submitted by Congressman Marsha Blackburn which were sent to me following my appearance before your Subcommittee on April 8, 2003. Please let me know if I can be of further assistance.

Sincerely,

Linda M. Springer
Controller

MAY-16-03 16:23 FROM:OMB ID: PAGE 1/4

EXECUTIVE OFFICE OF THE PRESIDENT
OFFICE OF MANAGEMENT AND BUDGET
OFFICE OF FEDERAL FINANCIAL MANAGEMENT
WASHINGTON, DC

FACSIMILE

Date: 5/16/03

Number of Pages: 3
(Excluding this cover sheet)

TO: Congressman Todd Platts

AGENCY/OFFICE: Subcommittee on Government Efficiency and financial mngmt

Telephone:

Fax: 225-2544

From: Linda Springer, Controller

Telephone: (202) 395-9161
Fax (202) 395-3174

Comments: Please direct any questions to Dana Ayers 395-9161.
Originals will be sent on monday.

What are your recommendations to arrest spending on Medicare / Medicaid and Social Security?

Structural changes to these programs are debated at high levels throughout the Administration and in Congress. From a financial management perspective, it is our responsibility to ensure these programs suffer from a minimal level of waste, fraud, and abuse. We are working hard to reduce erroneous payments in the Medicare program, which last year amounted to 6.3% of program payments or $13.3 billion. The Centers for Medicare and Medicaid Services are working to further reduce erroneous payments in the Medicare program by working with provider groups, such as the American Medical Association and the American Hospital Association, to clarify reimbursement rules and to impress upon health care providers the importance of fully documenting services.

Unfortunately, we don't yet have a Medicaid error rate. But because Medicaid makes more than $160 billion in payments annually, we are working hard with states to establish a methodology that could be used across the country to establish a uniform error rate. What we have found is not surprising. Insufficient documentation to support claims was a leading basis for classifying a payment as erroneous. Other errors include payments for medically unnecessary services or errors in coding, billing, or processing. Our effort to examine the integrity of Medicaid payments should reduce errors in these areas.

Social Security programs also must be vigilant about preventing fraud and error in their payments. In the Old- Age, Survivors and Disability Insurance program, SSA is working to ensure that payments are not made to prisoners or deceased beneficiaries. In the Supplemental Security Income Program, SSA is pursuing a number of initiatives to improve payment accuracy, including gaining easier access to bank account balance information; improving the quality of SSI adjudications, particularly redeterminations; and improving efficiency in identifying and processing changes that affect payments. These are part of the President's initiative to reduce erroneous payments throughout the federal government.

What is your recommended course of action to address the true cost of new legislation (for example, veterans' benefits, prescription drug plans)?

Estimating the true cost of public policy is challenging. But the shared stewardship responsibility of the Executive and Legislative Branches makes it imperative that we strive to enact legislation only when we have an adequate understanding of its true costs. I would recommend that Congress take a hard look at the accuracy of cost estimates made by the Congressional Budget Office vis a vis the true costs of programs after they are implemented. This performance-based assessment of CBO's performance could teach us a lot about how to improve our cost estimation techniques.

How are results being used to affect budgeting processes for the current and next year and how should they be used?

The Administration is accelerating the deadline for agencies to produce audited financial statements. For FY 2002 and FY 2003, agencies' combined performance and accountability reports are required and must be submitted to OMB and the Congress by February 1st. We are further accelerating the deadline for financial reporting so that by FY 2004 agencies will submit audited financial statements by November 15 and we will produce a Consolidated Financial Report on December 15. One of the principle reasons for this acceleration is so the Administration and Congress can use the information to make budgetary decisions.

GAO
Accountability * Integrity * Reliability

United States General Accounting Office
Washington, D.C. 20548

June 27, 2003

The Honorable Todd R. Platts
Chairman, Subcommittee on Government Efficiency
and Financial Management
Committee on Government Reform
House of Representatives

Subject: *Financial Management Systems: Core Financial Systems at the 24 Chief Financial Officers Act Agencies*

Dear Mr. Chairman:

On April 8, 2003, we testified before your Subcommittee on the fiscal year 2002 consolidated financial statements of the U.S. government.[1] In that testimony, we provided our perspectives on major issues relating to the U.S. government's consolidated financial statements for fiscal years 2001 and 2002, including impediments to rendering an audit opinion on consolidated financial statements. As a result of issues raised in our testimony about the preparation of the consolidated financial statements and the adequacy of financial management systems and controls at the 24 Chief Financial Officers (CFO) Act[2] agencies, you and other subcommittee members asked a number of questions about issues surrounding the consolidated financial statements. On June 16, 2003,[3] we responded to all but your question related to the status of financial management systems modernization agency by agency. As agreed with your office, the objectives

[1] U.S. General Accounting Office, *Fiscal Year 2002 U.S. Government Financial Statements: Sustained Leadership and Oversight Needed for Effective Implementation of Financial Management Reform*, GAO-03-572T (Washington, D.C.: Apr. 8, 2003).

[2] Pub. L. No. 101-576, 104 Stat. 2838 (1990). The Federal Emergency Management Agency (FEMA), one of the 24 CFO Act agencies, was transferred to the new Department of Homeland Security (DHS) effective March 1, 2003. With this transfer, FEMA will no longer be required to prepare and have audited stand-alone financial statements under the CFO Act. DHS, along with most other executive branch agencies, will be required to prepare and have audited financial statements under the Accountability of Tax Dollars Act of 2002, Pub. L. No. 107-289, 116 Stat. 2049 (Nov. 7, 2002). We did not include DHS in our review because of its unique status as a new agency as of March 1, 2003. We included FEMA in our review since FEMA was a CFO Act agency as of September 30, 2002, and because information on FEMA's core financial system will be useful as it is incorporated into DHS.

[3] U.S. General Accounting Office, *Responses to Posthearing Questions Related to GAO's Testimony on the U.S. Government's Consolidated Financial Statements for Fiscal Year 2002*, GAO-03-848R (Washington, D.C.: June 16, 2003).

of this letter, which address the remaining question, are to identify the core financial systems used at each of the CFO Act agencies as of September 30, 2002, and the status of any agency plans to update core financial systems. To do so, we used publicly available information and confirmed this information with the CFO Act agencies, but we did not validate or verify the information obtained or provided. Further details on our scope and methodology are provided on page 7.

Core Financial Systems

Core financial systems,[4] as defined by the Joint Financial Management Improvement Program (JFMIP),[5] include managing general ledger, funding, payments, receivables, and certain basic cost functions. The core financial systems receive data from other financial and feeder systems, such as acquisition, grant, and personnel systems, as well as from direct user input, and provide data for financial performance measurement and analysis and for financial statement preparation.

Enclosures I and II present detailed information on agencies' core financial systems including the software being used as of September 30, 2002, when the core financial systems were implemented, which agencies are planning to acquire new systems, and the target date for implementation of any new systems. Enclosure I includes 20 CFO Act agencies that reported they generally have in place a single core financial system for the agency and its subcomponent agencies and bureaus. In certain cases, more than one core financial system was used by the agencies. Enclosure II provides information on 4 agencies, the Departments of Defense (DOD), Justice (DOJ), the Treasury, and Health and Human Services (HHS), that reported having multiple core financial systems. Each of these 4 CFO Act agencies has 5 or more subcomponent agencies, which maintain separate core financial systems. However, the systems included in enclosures I and II may not include all of the JFMIP-defined functions of a core financial system.

[4] Joint Financial Management Improvement Program (JFMIP), *Core Financial Systems Requirements*, SR-02-01 (Washington, D.C.: November 2001).

[5] JFMIP is a joint and cooperative undertaking of the Office of Management and Budget, the Department of the Treasury, the Office of Personnel Management, and GAO, working with federal agencies to improve financial management practices throughout the government.

The following summary characteristics highlight key data included in enclosures I and II about the 24 CFO Act agencies' current and planned core financial systems as of September 30, 2002.

Core Financial Systems Software

The 24 CFO Act agencies used a variety of core financial systems software. Ten agencies used only commercial-off-the-shelf (COTS) software packages as their core financial systems.

- Two agencies, the Department of Education, and the Small Business Administration (SBA), exclusively used Oracle U.S. Federal Financials software.
- One agency, the Office of Personnel Management (OPM), exclusively used American Management Systems (AMS) Momentum software package.
- Four agencies, the Departments of Housing and Urban Development (HUD) and Veterans Affairs (VA), the Nuclear Regulatory Commission (NRC), and the Environmental Protection Agency (EPA), exclusively used AMS's Federal Financial System software package.
- Three agencies, the Department of Labor (DOL), the Federal Emergency Management Agency (FEMA), and the Social Security Administration (SSA), exclusively used other COTS packages.
- Three agencies, the Department of Energy (DOE), National Science Foundation (NSF), and the National Aeronautics and Space Administration (NASA), exclusively used custom software.
- Six agencies used a mix of 2 systems:
    - Five agencies had partially implemented a new system in a number of their respective bureaus as of September 30, 2002. These agencies were the Agency for International Development (AID); Departments of Transportation (DOT), State, and Agriculture (USDA); and the General Services Administration (GSA).
    - One agency, the Department of the Interior (DOI), used both a custom and a COTS software product.

- Five agencies used a variety of core financial systems.
  - DOD reported 100 core financial systems[6] in use in its subcomponent agencies and bureaus of its total systems inventory of 2,114 systems.
  - DOJ's subcomponent agencies used multiple core financial systems, ranging from custom-built software, to some of the more common software packages, such as those from AMS and SAP.
  - HHS's main subcomponent agencies used either the Arthur Young Federal Success software package or custom software.
  - Treasury's subcomponent agencies and bureaus used a variety of COTS packages, including AMS's Federal Financial System and Momentum products, SAP, and Peoplesoft Financials. One agency, the Bureau of the Public Debt (BPD), cross-serviced several other agencies within Treasury as well.
  - The Department of Commerce's (DOC) major subcomponent agencies used RELTEK's Federal Financial Management System—a modified COTS product. DOC's other agencies used either custom software or COTS products.

Age of the Core Financial Systems

The age of the core financial systems ranged from systems implemented in fiscal year 2002 to those implemented more than 30 years ago.

- Five agencies—Education, NRC, SBA, OPM, and NSF—have fully implemented new core financial systems since the beginning of fiscal year 2001.
- Four agencies—FEMA, HUD, SSA, and VA—have systems implemented from 2 to 10 years ago.
- Six agencies—DOC, AID, State, USDA, GSA, and DOT—were using both legacy systems and new core financial systems implemented in parts of the agencies as of September 30, 2002. For example, GSA used both a

[6] This list was compiled from DOD's "As Is Systems Inventory" as of October 31, 2002.

custom system originally implemented in 1974 and AMS Momentum that it was in the process of implementing as of September 30, 2002.

- Five agencies—NASA, DOE, DOI, DOL, and EPA—have systems that were implemented more than 10 years ago.
- Four agencies—DOD, DOJ, HHS, and Treasury—used multiple core financial systems that were implemented from the 1960s through 2001. For example, DOD has some core financial systems that were originally implemented in the 1960s and 1970s.

Software Selection Plans

Seventeen agencies[7] were planning to or were in the process of implementing new core financial systems as of September 30, 2002.

- Of this total, 11 have selected the software product they plan to use:
  - 3 have selected AMS Momentum (AID, GSA, and State),
  - 5 have selected Oracle U.S. Federal Financials (DOE, DOT, VA, HHS, and SSA),
  - 1 has selected RELTEK Federal Financial Management System (DOC),
  - 1 has selected SAP (NASA), and
  - 1 has selected AMS Federal Financial System (USDA).

[7] Treasury is among the agencies not planning to implement an agencywide core financial system. However, several of its subcomponent agencies are in the process of implementing core financial system software packages, including the Internal Revenue Service and the Office of the Comptroller of the Currency.

- The remaining 6 agencies have not reached the software selection phase of their acquisition process (DOD, DOI, DOJ, DOL, EPA, and HUD).
    - In DOD's case, a complete business systems[8] modernization project[9] is under way that proposes to revamp and integrate the systems used in DOD entities as part of a DOD-wide transformation.
    - DOJ plans to award a contract for the acquisition of a core software package in July 2003.

Target Implementation Dates

Target implementation dates for the 17 agencies planning to implement new core financial systems generally ranged from fiscal year 2003 to fiscal year 2008, though one agency had not yet selected a target implementation date.

- Three agencies plan to complete or have completed implementation in fiscal year 2003 (USDA, GSA, and NASA).
- Three agencies plan to complete their implementations in fiscal year 2004 (SSA, DOC, and DOT).
- Ten agencies have established target implementation dates ranging from 2 to 6 years in the future (AID, DOJ, DOL, HHS, EPA, HUD, VA, DOI, State, and DOE).
- One agency has not yet determined its target date for full implementation (DOD).

[8] Business systems include those that are used to support civilian personnel, finance, health, logistics, military personnel, procurement, and transportation.

[9] See U.S. General Accounting Office, *DOD Financial Management: Important Steps Underway But Reform Will Require a Long-term Commitment*, GAO-02-784T (Washington, D.C.: June 4, 2002); *DOD Business Systems Modernization: Continued Investment in Key Accounting Systems Needs to be Justified*, GAO-03-465 (Washington, D.C.: Mar. 28, 2003); *DOD Business Systems Modernization: Longstanding Management and Oversight Weaknesses Continue to Put Investments at Risk*, GAO-03-553T (Washington, D.C.: Mar. 31, 2003).

Life Cycle Phase

These 17 agencies were in different phases[10] of the process to implement a new core financial system as of September 30, 2002.

- Five agencies—HUD[11], DOI, DOL, DOD, and EPA—were in the *business modeling and requirements* phase.
- One agency—DOJ—was in the *analysis and design* phase.
- Three agencies were in the *development* phase: State which plans to implement an agencywide COTS product, DOE, which plans to implement a COTS-based product in October 2004, and VA, whose strategy includes a phased-in approach beginning in October 2003.
- Two agencies were in the *testing* phase: AID, which plans to implement the COTS software currently used domestically in its overseas regional offices, and HHS, which is using a phased rollout strategy with its subcomponent agencies.
- Six agencies—USDA, DOC, SSA, DOT, GSA, and NASA—were in the *deployment* phase as of September 30, 2002.

To identify and compile the status of CFO Act agencies' core financial systems, we reviewed publicly available information, including fiscal year 2002 performance and accountability reports for the CFO Act agencies, related reports by those agencies' Inspectors General (IG), as well as any reports that we issued on this matter. We reviewed other publicly available information, including agency, Office of Management and Budget (OMB), and JFMIP Web sites to identify information on current core financial systems and planned implementations. We also reviewed related OMB circulars, including A-127,[12] and JFMIP systems requirements for core financial systems and its *Framework for Federal Financial Management Systems.*[13] We shared the information we gathered on agencies' current

[10] See definition of life cycle phases in endnote 'a' of enclosure I.

[11] According to HUD, this phase will begin in July 2003.

[12] OMB Circular A-127, *Financial Management Systems*, as revised by Transmittal Memorandum No. 2, June 10, 1999.

[13] JFMIP, *Framework for Federal Financial Management Systems*, FFMSR-0 (Washington, D.C.: January 1995).

and planned systems with the agencies and obtained confirmations, corrections, or additional facts, but we did not independently validate or verify the information obtained or provided. We conducted our work from April to June 2003 in Washington, D.C.

We are sending copies of this letter to the Ranking Minority Member, Subcommittee on Government Efficiency and Financial Management, House Committee on Government Reform and the Chairman and Ranking Minority Member, Subcommittee on Financial Management, the Budget and International Security, Senate Committee on Governmental Affairs. Copies will be made available to others upon request. This letter will also be available at no charge on the GAO Web site at http://www.gao.gov.

If you have any questions about this letter, please contact me at (202) 512-9450 or thompsons@gao.gov or Kay Daly at (202) 512-9312 or dalykl@gao.gov. Key contributors to this letter were Adrien Atwood and Debra David. We look forward to working with you and your staff on related financial management systems issues.

Sincerely yours,

Sally E. Thompson
Director, Financial Management
and Assurance

Enclosures I and II

Enclosure I

Current and Planned Core Financial Systems at 20 CFO Act Agencies

	Core financial systems as of September 30, 2002			
Agency	**Name**	**Vendor and software name**	**COTS / modified COTS / custom**	**Implementation date**
Agency for International Development	Mission Accounting and Control System (MACS) used overseas / Phoenix	MACS-NA/Phoenix-AMS Momentum	MACS-Custom / Phoenix- COTS	MACS- June 1982/ Phoenix-December 2000
Department of Commerce	Commerce Administrative Management System (CAMS)[c]	CAMS- Savantage Solutions, Inc (Formerly RELTEK) Federal Financial Management System (FFMS)/Various (see endnote[c])	CAMS-Modified COTS/Various (see endnote[c])	Various (see endnote[c])
Department of Energy	Departmental Integrated Standardized Core Accounting System (DISCAS)	NA	Custom	April 1986
Department of the Interior	Federal Financial System (FFS) for 7 bureaus/offices and ABACIS for the other 2 bureaus	AMS Federal Financial System /ABACIS-NA	FFS-Modified COTS / ABACIS-Custom	FFS-1992 / ABACIS – early 1980s
Department of Labor	Department of Labor Accounting and Related Systems (DOLAR$)	Keane Federal Success	Modified COTS	October 1989
Deparmentt of Transportation	Departmental Accounting and Financial Information System (DAFIS) / Delphi	DAFIS-NA /Delphi – Oracle U.S. Federal Financials	DAFIS - Custom/ Delphi - Modified COTS	1982
Department of Education	Financial Management Systems Software (FMSS)	Oracle U.S. Federal Financials	COTS	January 2002
Environmental Protection Agency	Integrated Financial Management System (IFMS)	AMS Federal Financial System	Modified COTS	1988
Federal Emergency Management Agency	Integrated Financial Management Information System (IFMIS)	Digital Systems Group IFMIS	COTS	October 1995

Planned core financial systems after September 30, 2002

Plans to acquire new system?	Name of project/system	Vendor of new system and software	Planning start date	Target full implementation date	Life cycle phase [a]	Comments – mixed systems
Yes	AID plans to replace MACS with Phoenix	AMS Momentum	July 2003	October 2005 [b]	Testing phase	
Yes, ongoing	CAMS	RELTEK Federal Financial Management System [d]	1994	October 2003	Deployment phase	
Yes	I-MANAGE Standard Accounting System (STARS)	Oracle U.S. Federal Financials	March 1999	October 2004	Development phase	I-MANAGE program will integrate financials with human resources, budget formulation/execution, payroll, travel and procurement.
Yes	Financial and Business Management System (FBMS)	To be determined	2004	2008	Business modeling and requirements phase	FBMS project will support budget formulation, core financial, acquisition, travel, personal property/fleet management, real property, financial assistance, and enterprise management information functions.
Yes	To be determined	To be determined	2nd quarter of FY 2003	October 2006	Business modeling and requirements phase	DOL plans to implement a new managerial cost accounting system.
Yes, ongoing	Delphi	Oracle U.S. Federal Financials	1997	October 2003	Deployment phase	The Federal Aviation Administration is also in the process of implementing a labor distribution/cost accounting system.
No plans to acquire	NA	NA	NA	NA	NA	
Yes	Financial Replacement System (FinRS)	To be determined	October 2002	FY 2007	Business modeling and requirements phase	EPA also plans to replace its EPAYS and CPARS payroll systems and its MARS reporting system in FY 2003.
No plans to acquire	NA	NA	NA	NA	NA	As of March 2003, FEMA is part of the new Department of Homeland Security.

(Continued From Previous Page)

Core financial systems as of September 30, 2002

Agency	Name	Vendor and software name	COTS / modified COTS / custom	Implementation date
General Services Administration	National Electronic Accounting and Reporting (NEAR) / Pegasys	NEAR-NA /Pegasys - AMS Momentum	NEAR- Custom / Pegasys- COTS [e]	NEAR-1974 / Pegasys Phase I- June 2000
Department of Housing and Urban Development	HUD's Central Accounting Program System (HUDCAPS)	AMS Federal Financial System	Modified COTS	October 1998 for implementation as departmental general ledger
National Aeronautics and Space Administration	General Ledger Accounting System (GLAS) [g]	NA	Custom	1970s
Nuclear Regulatory Commission	Federal Financial System (FFS)	AMS Federal Financial System [i]	COTS	May 2002
National Science Foundation	Financial Accounting System	NA	Custom	April 2001
Office of Personnel Management	Government Financial Information System (GFIS)	AMS Momentum	COTS	August 2002
Small Business Administration	Joint Accounting and Administrative Management System (JAAMS)	Oracle U.S. Federal Financials	Modified COTS	October 2001
Social Security Administration	Financial Accounting System (FACTS)	Keane Federal Success	Modified COTS	October 1993
Department of State	Central Financial Management System (CFMS) /Regional Financial Management System (RFMS) [k]	CFMS – AMS Federal Financial System/RFMS - AMS Momentum	CFMS – COTS / RFMS - Modified COTS[l]	CFMS -1991
Department of Agriculture	Central Accounting System (CAS) / Foundation Financial Information System (FFIS)	CAS – NA / FFIS–AMS Federal Financial System	CAS - Custom / FFIS- Modified COTS	CAS-1976

Planned core financial systems after September 30, 2002

Plans to acquire new system?	Name of project/system	Vendor of new system and software	Planning start date	Target full implementation date	Life cycle phase [a]	Comments – mixed systems
Yes, ongoing	Pegasys	AMS Momentum	May 1998	October 2002	Deployment phase	Phase II includes the implementation of full accounts receivable, asset management and cost allocation by October 2004. Pegasys was the official core financial system at the end of October 2002.
Yes	HUD Integrated Financial Management Improvement Project (HIFMIP)	To be determined	July 2003	March 2007	Business modeling and requirements phase scheduled to begin in July 2003	Legacy insurance systems at the Federal Housing Administration (FHA) to be integrated by December 2006. [f]
Yes	Integrated Financial Management Program (IFMP)	SAP R/3	FY 2000	June 2003	Deployment phase[h]	
No plans to acquire	NA	NA	NA	NA	NA	NRC implemented a COTS-based cost accounting system in November 2002.[i]
No plans to acquire	NA	NA	NA	NA	NA	See endnote. [j]
No plans to acquire	NA	NA	NA	NA	NA	A cost allocation module will be added to GFIS with the first phase planned for implementation in September 2003.
No plans to acquire	NA	NA	NA	NA	NA	
Yes	Social Security Online Accounting and Reporting System	Oracle U.S. Federal Financials	June 2001 [k]	October 2003	Deployment phase	
Yes, ongoing	Global Financial Management System (GFMS)	AMS Momentum	June 1998	GFMS Domestic – FY 2005, Overseas – FY 2006	Development phase	
Yes, ongoing	FFIS	AMS Federal Financial System	NR	October 2002	Deployment phase	Beginning in December 2003, agency will start process for next core system implementation.

(Continued From Previous Page)

Core financial systems as of September 30, 2002

Agency	Name	Vendor and software name	COTS / modified COTS / custom	Implementation date
Department of Veterans Affairs	Financial Management System	AMS Federal Financial System	Modified COTS	September 1995

Planned core financial systems after September 30, 2002

Plans to acquire new system?	Name of project/system	Vendor of new system and software	Planning start date	Target full implementation date	Life cycle phase [a]	Comments – mixed systems
Yes	Core Financial and Logistics System (Core FLS)	Oracle U.S. Federal Financials	June 1999	March 2006	Development phase	VA has also selected the software to be used in the logistics module of the core financial system.

Legend

COTS – Commercial-off-the-shelf
NA – Not applicable
NR – No response

Source: GAO compiled.

[a]To help categorize the current status of agencies' systems implementation, we used the following system development life cycle phases: (1) *Business modeling and requirements* includes developing complete systems requirements, establishing the "as is" model of the business processes, and meeting with stakeholders. (2) *Analysis and design* addresses transforming the systems requirements into a design of the "to be" system. This phase would also include evaluation of vendor proposals and vendor selection. (3) *Development* involves the development and modification of the system software. (4) *Testing* covers verifying that all requirements have been correctly developed and tested and ensuring all identified defects have been documented and corrected. (5) *Deployment* includes training end users, converting data, putting the software into service, verifying that all requirements have been correctly implemented, and planning for the operations and support phase of software components. (6) *Operations and support* involves the monitoring of product integrity and ensuring the ongoing completeness and correctness of the system.

[b]AID and the State Department have agreed to integrate their separate Momentum applications into one application with two databases with full implementation expected in October 2005 following deployment of Phoenix to AID's overseas offices.

[c]The agencies and bureaus of the Department of Commerce, which had not implemented CAMS as of September 30, 2002, used other core financial systems, including custom systems (implemented in the 1980s), AMS Momentum (implemented in 2002) and cross-servicing with the Department of the Interior.

[d]Three Commerce bureaus will not implement CAMS, including the U.S. Patent and Trademark Office, the International Trade Administration, and the National Technical Information Service.

[e]According to GSA, all enhancements to the product were added to the baseline product by the vendor.

[f]Peoplesoft general ledger module implemented at FHA in October 2002.

[g]NASA has 9 centers, its headquarters offices and the Jet Propulsion Laboratory, each of which had its own custom-built financial systems until each center's conversion to the new core financial system in FY 2003.

[h]See U.S. General Accounting Office, *Business Modernization: Improvements Needed in Management of NASA's Integrated Financial Management Program*, GAO-03-507 (Washington, D.C.: Apr. 30, 2003).

[i]NRC's service provider for FFS is the Department of the Interior's National Business Center.

[j]This agency will adopt the Department of the Interior's personnel/payroll services in FY 2004.

[k]The solicitation for the software purchase was released in June 2001.

[l]CFMS accounts for State's domestic financial activity, while RFMS is for overseas activity.

[m]State uses a custom disbursement module in its regional financial management system.

Enclosure II

Current and Planned Core Financial Systems at 4 CFO Act Agencies

		Core financial systems as of September 30, 2002			
Agency	**Subagency**	**Name**	**Vendor and software name**	**COTS / modified COTS / custom**	**Implementation date**
Department of Defense		100 core systems [b]	Various	Various	1960s, 1970s, 1980s, and 1990s
Department of Justice [c]	DOJ	No consolidated core financial system	NA	NA	NA
Department of Justice	BOP	Financial Management Information System (FMIS2)	NA	Custom	October 1999
Department of Justice	OJP	Integrated Financial Management Information System (IFMIS)	Digital Systems Group- Financial Management System Software	Modified COTS	December 1998
Department of Justice	INS	Financial Accounting Control System (FACS)/Federal Financial Management System (FFMS)	FACS – NA/ Savantage Solutions, Inc. (formerly REL-TEK) -FFMS	FACS – Custom /FFMS – Modified COTS	October 1997
Department of Justice	FPI	Millennium System	SAP	Modified COTS	May 2000
Department of Justice	DEA	Federal Financial System (FFS)	Cross-serviced by DOI	Modified COTS	October 1998
Department of Justice	FBI	Financial Management System (FMS)	Geac Computer Corporation Limited, Geac Enterprise Server E Series	Modified COTS	October 1985
Department of Justice	OBDs	FMIS2	NA	Custom	December 2002

Planned core financial systems after September 30, 2002						
Plans to acquire new system?	**Name of project / system**	**Vendor of new system and software**	**Planning start date**	**Target full implementation date**	**Life cycle phase [a]**	**Comments - mixed systems**
Yes	Not yet decided	To be determined	Varies	To be determined	Business modeling and requirements phase	Implementation of a core financial system(s) for DOD is a long-term effort due to the significant number of systems and complexity of the Department.
Yes	United Financial Management System Project (UFMS)	To be determined	April 2002	October 2007	Analysis and design phase	COTS award projected – July 2003. Implementation and integration contract to follow. UFMS includes integrated procurement & e-travel solutions.
Part of UFMS Implementation	UFMS	To be determined	October 2004	October 2006	Analysis and design phase	
Part of UFMS Implementation	UFMS	To be determined	October 2004	October 2006	Analysis and design phase	
NA	NA	NA	NA	NA	NA	In March 2003, INS was transferred to the Department of Homeland Security.
No plans to acquire	NA	NA	NA	NA	NA	Current COTS satisfies commercial/manufacturing business requirements unique to FPI. FPI is not included in UFMS Project.
Part of UFMS Implementation	UFMS	To be determined	October 2003	October 2005	Analysis and design phase	
Part of UFMS Implementation	UFMS	To be determined	August 2002	October 2004	Analysis and design phase	
Part of UFMS Implementation	UFMS	To be determined	October 2005	October 2007	Analysis and design phase	Also supports the Working Capital Fund and Asset Forfeiture Fund/Seized Asset Deposit Fund reporting entities.

(Continued From Previous Page)

Core financial systems as of September 30, 2002

Agency	Subagency	Name	Vendor and software name	COTS / modified COTS / custom	Implementation date
Department of Justice	USMS	Standardized Tracking Accounting and Reporting System (STARS) at headquarters, Financial Management System (FMS) used by district offices	STARS -ieFARS - ACS Government Solutions Group /FMS – NA	STARS –Modified COTS/FMS – Custom	October 1997
Department of Health and Human Services [d]	HHS	NA	NA	NA	NA
Department of Health and Human Services	PSC	CORE	Arthur Young–Federal Success	Modified COTS	1992
Department of Health and Human Services	FDA	General Ledger Accounting System (GLAS)	NA	Custom	FY1968-FY1969
Department of Health and Human Services	CDC	Total On-Line Processing System (TOPS)	Arthur Young–Federal Success	Modified COTS	1991
Department of Health and Human Services	NIH	Central Accounting System (CAS)	NA	Custom	Mid-1970s
Department of Health and Human Services	CMS	Financial Accounting and Control System (FACS)	Arthur Young–Federal Success	Modified COTS	1980s
Department of the Treasury [e]	Treasury	No consolidated core financial system[f]	NA	NA	NA
Department of the Treasury	BPD	Federal Financial System (FFS)	American Management Systems (AMS) Federal Financial System (FFS)	COTS	October 1994

Planned core financial systems after September 30, 2002

Plans to acquire new system?	Name of project / system	Vendor of new system and software	Planning start date	Target full implementation date	Life cycle phase [a]	Comments - mixed systems
Part of UFMS Implementation	UFMS	To be determined	October 2003	October 2005	Analysis and design phase	
Yes	Unified Financial Management System (UFMS)	Oracle U.S. Federal Financials	July 2001	April 2007	Testing phase	
Part of the UFMS implementation	UFMS	Oracle U.S. Federal Financials	January 2004	April 2007	Development phase	
Part of the UFMS implementation	Financial Enterprise Solutions (FES)	Oracle U.S. Federal Financials	July 2003	May 2005	Development phase	FES is the FDA-named project that is part of the full UFMS implementation.
Part of the UFMS implementation	UFMS	Oracle U.S. Federal Financials	October 2002	October 2004	Development phase	
Part of the UFMS implementation	NIH's Business and Research Support System (NBRSS)	Oracle U.S. Federal Financials	1999	October 2002	Deployment phase	NBRSS is the NIH-named project that is part of the full UFMS implementation.
Part of the UFMS implementation	Healthcare Integrated General Ledger Accounting System (HIGLAS)	Oracle U.S. Federal Financials	2000	September 2007	Development phase	HIGLAS is a second component of UFMS. HIGLAS is a separate core system from the one used by other subagencies.
No plans to acquire	NA	NA	NA	NA	NA	
Yes	Oracle U.S. Federal Financials	Oracle U.S. Federal Financials	NR	October 2002	Deployment phase	BPD implemented the Compusearch acquisition application "Prism" in January 2002

(Continued From Previous Page)

Core financial systems as of September 30, 2002

Agency	Subagency	Name	Vendor and software name	COTS / modified COTS / custom	Implementation date
Department of the Treasury	ATF	Financial Resources Desktop (FRED)	AMS Momentum	Modified COTS	October 1999
Department of the Treasury	BEP	BEP Management Information System (BEPMIS)	SSA Global Technologies CAS	COTS	1984
Department of the Treasury	USCS	FFS and SAP R/3 Phase I	AMS FFS /SAP R/3	FFS -Modified COTS/SAP - Modified COTS	FFS - October 1992 /SAP - April 2002
Department of the Treasury	DO	FFS	AMS FFS	COTS	BPD began cross-servicing DO in February 2001
Department of the Treasury	FinCEN	FFS/ SAP R/3 Phase I	AMS FFS / SAP R/3	FFS -Modified COTS/SAP - Modified COTS	FinCEN is cross-serviced by USCS
Department of the Treasury	IRS	Automated Financial Systems (AFS)	AMS FFS	Modified COTS	October 1992

Planned core financial systems after September 30, 2002						
Plans to acquire new system?	**Name of project / system**	**Vendor of new system and software**	**Planning start date**	**Target full implementation date**	**Life cycle phase [a]**	**Comments - mixed systems**
NA						This bureau was transferred to the Department of Justice in 2003.
No plans to acquire	NA	NA	NA	NA	NA	
Yes, ongoing	SAP R/3 Release II and III	SAP R/3	1995	Release II is scheduled for implementation in October 2003 and will include procurement and asset management capabilities. The scheduled implementation date for Release III is October 2004, but this date is subject to review by the Department of Homeland Security (DHS).	Deployment phase	This bureau was transferred to DHS. An accounts receivable subsidiary ledger that will support the Automated Commercial Environment (ACE) is scheduled for implementation in March 2004, but this date is subject to review by DHS.
Yes	Oracle U.S. Federal Financials	Oracle U.S. Federal Financials	October 2003	BPD will begin cross-servicing DO using Oracle in October 2003.	Testing phase	BPD will begin cross-servicing DO to use the Compusearch acquisition application "Prism" in October 2003.
No plans to acquire	NA	NA	NA	NA	NA	USCS staff use FFS and SAP R/3 to perform FinCEN's financial management activities.
Yes	Integrated Financial System	SAP R/3	October 2000	Release 1: October 2003	Testing phase	Release 1 will include core financial functionality. Release 2, to be implemented in August 2005, will include asset management functionality.

(Continued From Previous Page)

			Core financial systems as of September 30, 2002		
Agency	**Subagency**	**Name**	**Vendor and software name**	**COTS / modified COTS / custom**	**Implementation date**
Department of the Treasury	FMS	FFS	AMS FFS	COTS	BPD began cross-servicing FMS in June 1999
Department of the Treasury	OTS	FFS	AMS FFS	COTS	BPD began cross-servicing OTS in October 2002
Department of the Treasury	USSS	Financial Management and Accounting System (FMAS)	Keane Federal Success	Modified COTS	October 1988

Planned core financial systems after September 30, 2002						
Plans to acquire new system?	**Name of project / system**	**Vendor of new system and software**	**Planning start date**	**Target full implementation date**	**Life cycle phase [a]**	**Comments - mixed systems**
Yes	Oracle U.S. Federal Financials	Oracle U.S. Federal Financials (cross-serviced by BPD)	February 2003	BPD will begin cross-servicing FMS in October 2003	Testing phase	
Yes	Oracle U.S. Federal Financials	Oracle U.S. Federal Financials (cross-serviced by BPD)	NR	BPD will begin cross-servicing OTS in October 2004	Business modeling and requirements phase	
Yes	Enterprise Financial Management System (EFMS)	Oracle U.S. Federal Financials	August 2001	April 2004	Development phase	This bureau was transferred to DHS in March 2003.

Legend

COTS - Commercial-off-the-shelf
NA - Not applicable
NR - No response

Source: GAO compiled.

[a]To help categorize the current status of agencies' systems implementation, we used the following system development lifecycle phases: (1) *Business modeling and requirements* includes developing complete systems requirements, establishing the "as-is" model of the business processes and meeting with stakeholders. (2) *Analysis and design* addresses transforming the systems requirements into a design of the "to-be" system. This phase would also include evaluation of vendor proposals and vendor selection. (3) *Development* involves the development and modification of the system software. (4) *Testing* covers verifying that all requirements have been correctly developed and tested and ensuring all identified defects have been documented and corrected. (5) *Deployment* includes training end users, converting data, putting the software into service, verifying that all requirements have been correctly implemented and planning for the operations and support phase of software components. (6) *Operations and support* involves the monitoring of product integrity and ensuring the ongoing completeness and correctness of system.

[b]DOD is still reviewing and analyzing its systems inventory as part of its business systems modernization and therefore, this list may or may not be complete. This list was compiled from DOD's "As Is Systems Inventory" as of October 31, 2002.

[c]Department of Justice: BOP: Bureau of Prisons, OJP: Office of Justice Programs, INS: Immigration and Naturalization Service, FPI: Federal Prisons Industries, Inc, DEA: Drug Enforcement Agency, FBI: Federal Bureau of Investigation, OBDs: Offices, Boards and Divisions, USMS: United States Marshals Service.

[d]Department of Health and Human Services: PSC: Program Support Center, FDA: Food and Drug Administration, CDC: Centers for Disease Control and Prevention, NIH: National Institutes of Health, CMS: Centers for Medicare and Medicaid Services.

[e]Department of Treasury: BPD: Bureau of the Public Debt, ATF: Alcohol, Tobacco and Firearms, BEP: Bureau of Engraving and Printing, USCS: United States Customs Service, DO: Departmental Offices, FinCEN: Financial Crimes Enforcement Network, IRS: Internal Revenue Service, FMS: Financial Management Service, OTS: Office of Thrift Supervision, USSS: United States Secret Service. Treasury's other bureaus, not included above, used a variety of COTS packages.

[f]Although Treasury does not have an agencywide core financial system, it does utilize automated tools and a central data warehouse for analysis and reporting.

GAO's Mission

The General Accounting Office, the audit, evaluation and investigative arm of Congress, exists to support Congress in meeting its constitutional responsibilities and to help improve the performance and accountability of the federal government for the American people. GAO examines the use of public funds; evaluates federal programs and policies; and provides analyses, recommendations, and other assistance to help Congress make informed oversight, policy, and funding decisions. GAO's commitment to good government is reflected in its core values of accountability, integrity, and reliability.

Obtaining Copies of GAO Reports and Testimony

The fastest and easiest way to obtain copies of GAO documents at no cost is through the Internet. GAO's Web site (www.gao.gov) contains abstracts and full-text files of current reports and testimony and an expanding archive of older products. The Web site features a search engine to help you locate documents using key words and phrases. You can print these documents in their entirety, including charts and other graphics.

Each day, GAO issues a list of newly released reports, testimony, and correspondence. GAO posts this list, known as "Today's Reports," on its Web site daily. The list contains links to the full-text document files. To have GAO e-mail this list to you every afternoon, go to www.gao.gov and select "Subscribe to e-mail alerts" under the "Order GAO Products" heading.

Order by Mail or Phone

The first copy of each printed report is free. Additional copies are $2 each. A check or money order should be made out to the Superintendent of Documents. GAO also accepts VISA and Mastercard. Orders for 100 or more copies mailed to a single address are discounted 25 percent. Orders should be sent to:

U.S. General Accounting Office
441 G Street NW, Room LM
Washington, D.C. 20548

To order by Phone: Voice: (202) 512-6000
TDD: (202) 512-2537
Fax: (202) 512-6061

To Report Fraud, Waste, and Abuse in Federal Programs

Contact:

Web site: www.gao.gov/fraudnet/fraudnet.htm
E-mail: fraudnet@gao.gov
Automated answering system: (800) 424-5454 or (202) 512-7470

Public Affairs

Jeff Nelligan, Managing Director, NelliganJ@gao.gov (202) 512-4800
U.S. General Accounting Office, 441 G Street NW, Room 7149
Washington, D.C. 20548

PRINTED ON RECYCLED PAPER